GW01374361

A POCKETFUL OF STORIES FOR FIVE YEAR OLDS

Also available from Pat Thomson,
and published by Doubleday:

A BUCKETFUL OF STORIES
FOR SIX YEAR OLDS

A BASKET OF STORIES
FOR SEVEN YEAR OLDS

A SACKFUL OF STORIES
FOR EIGHT YEAR OLDS

A CHEST OF STORIES
FOR NINE YEAR OLDS

A Pocketful of Stories for Five Year Olds

COLLECTED BY PAT THOMSON

Illustrated by Penny Dann

DOUBLEDAY
LONDON • NEW YORK • TORONTO • SYDNEY • AUCKLAND

TRANSWORLD PUBLISHERS LTD
61-63 Uxbridge Road, London W5 5SA

TRANSWORLD PUBLISHERS (AUSTRALIA) PTY LTD
15-23 Helles Avenue, Moorebank, NSW 2170

TRANSWORLD PUBLISHERS (NZ) LTD
Cnr Moselle and Waipareira Aves,
Henderson, Auckland

DOUBLEDAY CANADA LTD
105 Bond Street, Toronto, Ontario M5B 1Y3

Published 1991 by Doubleday
a division of Transworld Publishers Ltd

Collection copyright © 1991 by Pat Thomson
Illustrations copyright © 1991 by Penny Dann

The right of Pat Thomson to be identified as the Author
of this work has been asserted in accordance with
the Copyright, Designs and Patents Act 1988

A catalogue record for this book is available
from the British Library

ISBN 0 385 402376

All rights reserved. No part of this publication may
be reproduced, stored in a retrieval system, or
transmitted in any form or by any means,
electronic, mechanical, photocopying, recording,
or otherwise, without the prior permission of
the publishers

This book is sold subject to the
Standard Conditions of Sale of Net Books
and may not be re-sold in the U.K. below the net price
fixed by the publishers for the book.

Printed in Great Britain by
Mackays of Chatham plc, Chatham, Kent

Acknowledgements

The editor and publisher are grateful for permission to include the following copyright material in this anthology:

Anon, 'The Magic Broom' (original title 'Phillipippa') from *My Holiday Book*, ed. Mrs Herbert Strang (OUP, 1936). Reprinted by permission of Oxford University Press.

Paul Biegel, 'The Naughty Shoes'. Reprinted by permission of the author.

Lucy Boston, 'The House That Grew', © L.M. Boston, 1969. First published in 1969 by Faber & Faber Ltd.

Jean Chapman, 'The Lord of the Golden Umbrellas' from *Velvet Paws and Whiskers* (Hodder, 1979). Text © Jean Chapman, 1979. Reprinted by permission of the author.

Louise Fatio, 'The Happy Lion'. First published in Great Britain by The Bodley Head, 1955. Copyright Louise Fatio Duvoisin & Roger Duvoisin, 1954.

Alan Garner, 'The Girl and the Geese'. Text © Alan Garner, 1985. First published by Fontana. Used by permission of David Higham Associates Ltd.

David Harrison, 'The Giant Who Threw Tantrums' from *The Book of Giant Stories* (Cape, 1972). Text © David Harrison, 1972. Reprinted by permission of Random Century Group.

Margaret Joy, 'Mr Gill Makes a Wish' from *Allotment Lane School Again*. © Margaret Joy, 1985. First published by Faber & Faber, 1985.

Astrid Lindgren, 'The Tomten' (Viking Kestrel, 1985). © Astrid Lindgren, 1962. Reprinted by permission of Penguin Book Ltd.

Arnold Lobel, 'Strange Bumps' from *Owl at Home*. © 1975 by Arnold Lobel (World's Work Ltd). Reprinted by permission of Octopus Publishing Group Library.

Joan G. Robinson, 'Teddy Robinson and the China Gnome' from *Dear Teddy Robinson*. © Joan G. Robinson, 1956. Reprinted by permission of Harrap Publishing Group Ltd.

David Thomson, 'Danny Fox Steals Some Fish' from *Danny Fox* (Kestrel Books, 1966). © David Thomson, 1966. Reprinted by permission of Penguin Books Ltd.

Pat Thomson, 'Ticky Picky Boom Boom, an Ananse Story' retold by Pat Thomson. © Pat Thomson, 1991. Used with permission.

Joanna Troughton, 'Ombungo-rombunga' (original title 'Tortoise's Dream'). © Joanna Troughton, 1980. Reprinted by permission of Blackie & Son Ltd.

Alison Uttley, 'The Riddle-Me-Ree' from *The Adventures of Tim Rabbit* (Faber & Faber Ltd).

Jeanne Willis, 'The Long Blue Blazer', illustrated by Susan Varley. Reprinted by permission of Andersen Press Ltd.

Every effort has been made to trace and contact copyright holders before publication. If any errors or omissions occur the pubisher will be pleased to rectify these at the earliest opportunity.

CONTENTS

Mr Gill Makes a Wish
by Margaret Joy   1

The Giant Who Threw Tantrums
by David L. Harrison   10

Strange Bumps
by Arnold Lobel   18

Ticky Picky Boom Boom
an Ananse story told by Pat Thomson   21

The Happy Lion
by Louise Fatio   30

The Girl and the Geese
by Alan Garner   39

The Sing-Song of Old Man Kangaroo
by Rudyard Kipling   47

The Naughty Shoes
a Dutch story by Paul Biegel   58

The House That Grew
by Lucy Boston   66

The Magic Broom
Anon.   83

Teddy Robinson and the China Gnome
by Joan G. Robinson   91

Omumbo-rombonga
a retelling of the traditional tale by Joanna Troughton   110

The Riddle-Me-Ree
by Alison Uttley   119

The Tomten
by Astrid Lindgren   133

Danny Fox Steals Some Fish
by David Thomson   141

The Long, Blue Blazer
by Jeanne Willis   156

Lord of the Golden Umbrellas
by Jean Chapman   161

A POCKETFUL OF STORIES FOR FIVE YEAR OLDS

Mr Gill Makes a Wish

Mr Gill was busy in his office. He was sitting behind his big desk, thinking about Allotment Lane School and all the jobs that needed to be done.

First of all there was the hole in the roof. Every time it rained, the Big Boys and Girls in the top class had to put buckets and cloths on the floor to catch the drops that dripped down through the ceiling on to the floor of their classroom.

And today the sky looked *very* dark and cloudy. Mr Gill felt sure the rain would soon come pouring down – on to the roof, then in through the ceiling, then drip, drip, drip on to the floor. Oh dear! He sneezed a very loud sneeze.

'And another thing that's bothering me,' thought Mr Gill to himself, 'is the dinner trays. Some of the children seem to be butterfingers these days. They stand in the line for dinners, chatting to their friends and forgetting that they're holding their plastic tray ready for dinner. Then – C-R-A-S-H! Everyone jumps and looks round – another tray is broken, or at least cracked. Then I have to order more new trays.'

Mr Gill sneezed two very loud sneezes, then looked at the pile of letters on his desk.

'Have I got to answer all these?' he groaned. He was talking to himself, and it was a silly question, because he knew he had to, just as he knew that later on he had to talk to Mr Loftus the caretaker about the broken window in the kitchen; someone had kicked a football through it by mistake.

Then he knew he had to phone the school photographer who was coming to take photographs of the children. After that, Mr Loftus was going to show him two broken chairs – so that would mean ordering two new ones. Then one of the children's mothers was coming to see him because her little boy wasn't getting on with his reading, and she wanted to find out why. After that, one of the fathers was coming to see him because he thought there was too much fighting in the playground. Miss Mee was coming to see him to ask for some money to buy new books for the school library; then Mrs Owthwaite's children were going to show him how well they were getting on with their number work. And Mr Gill knew that some children in Class 3 had promised to come and show him the big fat toad they had found on the school field. Later on, when Mrs Hubb, the school secretary, had counted all the dinner money, he would have to drive with it to the bank.

Mr Gill thought it all sounded like a *very* busy morning.

'Oh dear, oh dear!' he said, and sneezed three very loud sneezes, so that his eyes watered and the walls shook. In the next room Mrs Hubb put her hands over her ears.

'And I think I've got a cold coming

too,' said Mr Gill to himself. He blew his nose very noisily and looked out of the window: it was pouring with rain.

'Oh no,' said poor Mr Gill, 'not rain! That's the limit, the absolute limit! Just for today, I wish . . . I wish that everyone in the school would *disappear* and leave me alone!'

He sat for five minutes holding his aching head in his hands. He sighed and sneezed four very loud sneezes, then started to read his pile of letters.

'There,' he said, half an hour later and much more cheerful. 'I've read all those letters. I'll just go and ask Mrs Hubb if she'll type the answers to them.'

He went next door into her tiny office – but she wasn't there. 'That's funny,' thought Mr Gill. 'Never mind, I'll go and see if the rain's come through the ceiling in the top class.'

He walked along to the classroom and noticed a damp patch on the ceiling, but there wasn't a pool of water on the floor, so this made him even more cheerful.

'But where are the children?' he suddenly wondered. There was no sign of the children or their teacher. Everything was strangely quiet.

'That's very odd indeed,' thought Mr Gill, feeling a little less cheerful after all. 'I'd better go and look in all the other classrooms.'

He did. He looked into every single room, and every single room was *completely* empty. There wasn't another person to be seen. Everything was absolutely silent.

'Oh my goodness,' said Mr Gill. 'What was it I said earlier? I wish that everyone in the school would *disappear and leave me alone*. And now they have! My wish has come true. I've lost everyone in the school! Oh dear, oh dear, oh dear!'

And he sneezed five extremely loud sneezes.

'What shall I tell Mr Hubb has happened to his wife? What shall I tell the teachers' husbands and wives? How can I tell all the mothers and fathers that their children have disappeared? Oh dear, oh dear!'

Mr Gill's head was aching so much that he thought he'd better go outside for some fresh air. He looked out of the window. The rain had stopped and the sun had come out. He stepped out of the school door and into the playground – and stood still.

There, in the middle of the playground was Mrs Hubb, *and* all the children from all the classes, *and* all their teachers. Mr Gill suddenly felt very relieved that he hadn't made them all disappear with his silly wish.

'*There* you all are, thank goodness,' he said, but nobody heard him – they were all looking up at the sky. Mr Gill shaded his eyes against the bright sunshine.

'What is it?' he asked.

'A rainbow,' said Mrs Hubb. 'Isn't it beautiful? Look – it stretches right across the sky, right over Allotment Lane School. All the teachers wanted to bring the children outside to see such a beautiful rainbow, and so I thought I'd come out too.'

She looked at Mr Gill and said, 'But we didn't disturb you, because we knew you were very busy – I hope you didn't think we'd disappeared, did you?'

'Um . . . er . . . no, no, of course not. Of course not,' said Mr Gill quickly. 'But I'm glad I've seen the rainbow. It's made me feel quite cheerful again. Even my cold feels a little better.'

He smiled at everyone. Then he gave one more sneeze – just a little one this time – and went back to his room.

This story is by Margaret Joy.

The Giant Who Threw Tantrums

At the foot of Thistle Mountain lay a village.

In the village lived a little boy who liked to go walking. One Saturday afternoon he was walking in the woods when he was startled by a terrible noise.

He scrambled quickly behind a bush.

Before long a huge giant came stamping down the path.

He looked upset.

'Tanglebangled ringlepox!' the giant bellowed. He banged his head against a tree until the leaves shook off like snowflakes.

'Franglewhangled whippersnack!' the giant roared. Yanking up the tree, he whirled it around his head and knocked down twenty-seven other trees.

Muttering to himself, he stalked up the path towards the top of Thistle Mountain.

The little boy hurried home.

'I just saw a giant throwing a tantrum!' he told everyone in the village.

They only smiled.

'There's no such thing as a giant,' the mayor assured him.

'He knocked down twenty-seven trees,' said the little boy.

'Must have been a tornado,' the weatherman said with a nod. 'Happens around here all the time.'

The next Saturday afternoon the little boy again went walking. Before long he heard a horrible noise. Quick as lightning, he slipped behind a tree.

Soon the same giant came storming down the path. He still looked upset.

'Pollywogging frizzelsnatch!' he yelled. Throwing himself down, he pounded the ground with both fists.

Boulders bounced like hailstones.

Scowling, the giant puckered his lips into an 'O'.

He drew in his breath sharply. It sounded like somebody slurping soup.

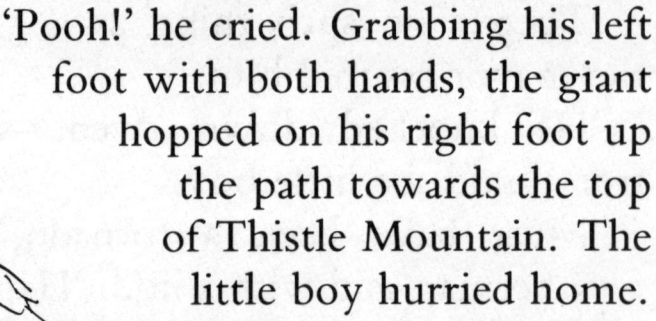

'Pooh!' he cried. Grabbing his left foot with both hands, the giant hopped on his right foot up the path towards the top of Thistle Mountain. The little boy hurried home.

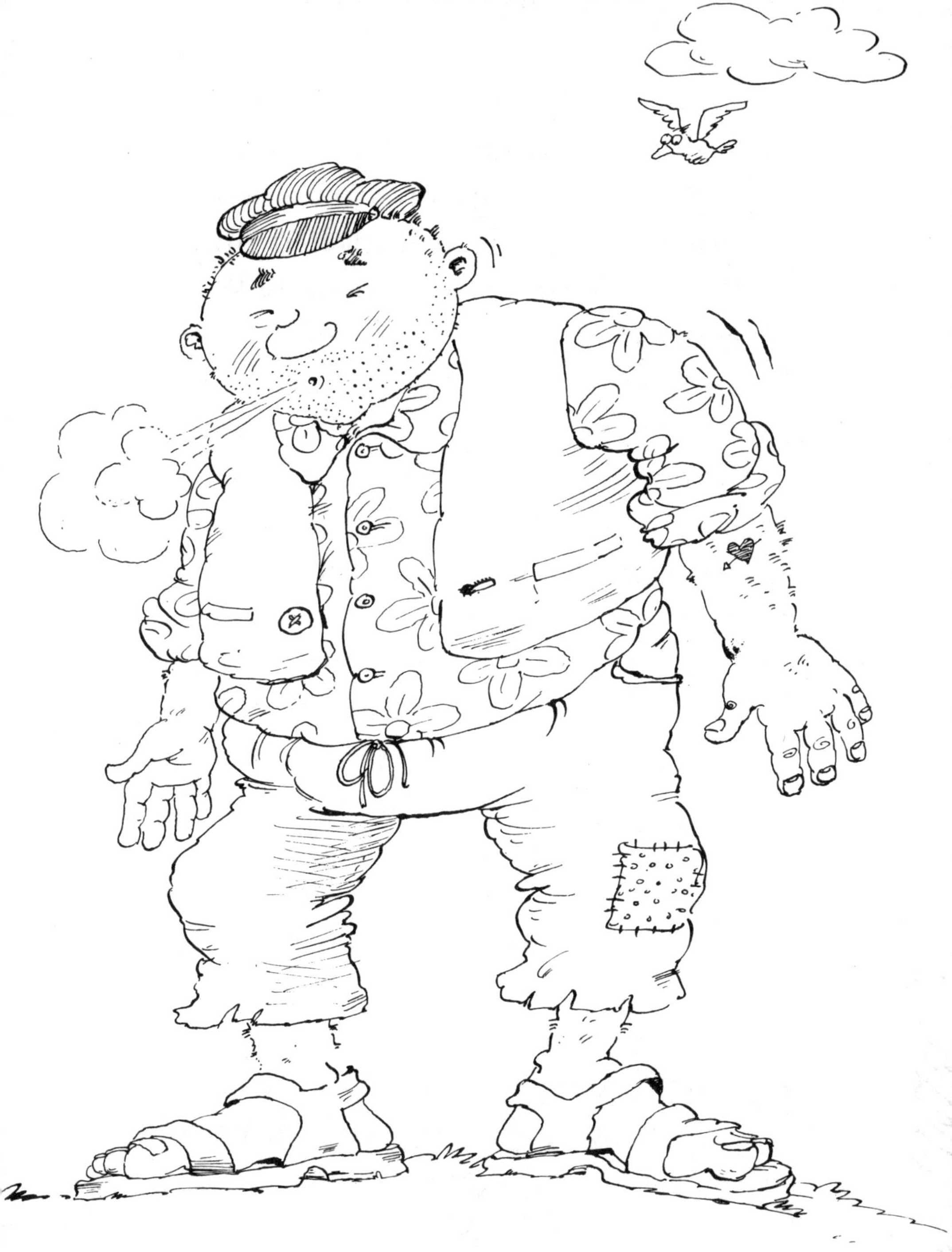

'That giant's at it again,' he told everyone. 'He threw such a tantrum that the ground trembled!'

'Must have been an earthquake,' the police chief said. 'Happens around here sometimes.'

The next Saturday afternoon the little boy again went walking. Before long he heard a frightening noise.

He dropped down behind a rock.

Soon the giant came fuming down the path. When he reached the little boy's rock, he puckered his lips into an 'O'. He drew in his breath sharply with a loud, rushing-wind sound. 'Phooey!' he cried. 'I *never* get it right!'

The giant held his breath until his face turned blue and his eyes rolled up. 'Fozzlehumper backawacket!' he panted. Then he lumbered up the path towards the top of Thistle Mountain.

The little boy followed him. Up

and up and up he climbed to the very top of Thistle Mountain.

There he discovered a huge cave. A surprising sound was coming from it. The giant was crying!

'All I want is to whistle,' he sighed through his tears. 'But every time I try, it comes out wrong!'

The little boy had just learned to whistle. He knew how hard it could be. He stepped inside the cave.

The giant looked surprised. 'How did *you* get here?'

'I know what you're doing wrong,' the little boy said.

When the giant heard that, he leaned down and put his hands on his knees.

'Tell me at once!' he begged.

'You have to stop throwing tantrums,' the little boy told him.

'I promise!' said the giant, who didn't want anyone to think he had poor manners.

'Pucker your lips . . .' the little boy said.

'I always do!' the giant assured him.

'Then blow,' the little boy added.

'Blow?'

'Blow.'

The giant looked as if he didn't believe it. He puckered his lips into an 'O'. He blew. Out came a long, low whistle. It sounded like a railway engine. The giant smiled.

He shouted, 'I whistled! Did you hear that? I whistled!'

Taking the little boy's hand, he danced in a circle.

'You're a good friend,' the giant said.

'Thank you,' said the little boy. 'Perhaps some time we can whistle together. But just now I have to go. It's my suppertime.'

The giant stood before his cave and waved good-bye.

The little boy seldom saw the giant after that. But the giant kept his promise about not throwing tantrums.

'We never have earthquakes,' the mayor liked to say.

'Haven't had a tornado in ages,' the weatherman would add.

Now and then they heard a long, low whistle somewhere in the distance.

'Must be a train,' the police chief would say.

But the little boy knew his friend the giant was walking up the path towards the top of Thistle Mountain – whistling.

This story is by David L. Harrison.

Strange Bumps

Owl was in bed.

'It is time to blow out the candle and go to sleep,' he said with a yawn.

Then Owl saw two bumps under the blanket at the bottom of his bed.

'What can those strange bumps be?' asked Owl.

Owl lifted up the blanket. He looked down into the bed. All he could see was darkness. Owl tried to sleep, but he could not.

'What if those two strange bumps grow bigger and bigger while I am asleep?' said Owl. 'That would not be pleasant.'

Owl moved his right foot up and down. The bump on the right moved up and down.

'One of those bumps is moving!' said Owl.

Owl moved his left foot up and down. The bump on the left moved up and down.

'The other bump is moving!' cried Owl.

Owl pulled all of the covers off his bed. The bumps had gone. All Owl could see at the bottom of the bed were his own two feet.

'But now I am cold,' said Owl. 'I will cover myself with the blankets again.'

As soon as he did, he saw the same two bumps.

'Those bumps are back!' shouted Owl. 'Bumps, bumps, bumps! I will never sleep tonight!'

Owl jumped up and down on top of his bed.

'Where are you? What are you?' he cried. With a crash and a bang the bed came falling down.

Owl ran down the stairs. He sat in his chair near the fire.

'I will let those two strange bumps sit on my bed all by themselves,' said Owl. 'Let them grow as big as they wish. I will sleep right here where I am safe.'

And that is what he did.

This story is by Arnold Lobel.

Ticky Picky Boom Boom

Ananse the trickster had a very fine vegetable garden. He had every vegetable imaginable; plenty of potatoes and more yams than he could eat. But there was one thing he did not have: a flower garden, and Ananse wanted above all to have flowers, just like a rich man.

'I shall turn the yam patch into a flower garden,' he decided, 'and I shall make Mr Tiger dig the flower bed for me.'

Now Mr Tiger had been tricked by Ananse before and he was cautious.

'What will you give me if I dig out the yams?' he asked.

'You may keep all the yams you dig up,' replied Ananse.

Mr Tiger was satisfied with that. He loved to eat yams. So, early next morning, he began to dig Ananse's garden for him. All day, he dug and dug, but the harder he worked, the deeper the yams seemed to sink into the ground. By the end of the day, Ananse's garden was thoroughly turned over, but Mr Tiger had not been able to get any yams for himself at all.

Mr Tiger was hot, tired and furious. This was another of Ananse's tricks! He lost his temper and chopped at one of the yams. He chopped it into little pieces, and then set off for home, muttering angrily.

What was that?

Behind him, Mr Tiger heard a

noise. A shuffling noise at first and then a stamping of small feet. Mr Tiger turned around – and along the road behind him, walking on little vegetable legs, came the yams! The noise that their feet made went like this:

    Ticky picky boom boom
    Ticky picky boom boom
    Ticky picky boom boom bouf!

Tiger began to run.
The yams began to run, too.
Tiger began to gallop.
The yams began to gallop.
Tiger jumped.
The yams jumped.
  Mr Tiger made straight for Mr Dog's house, running as fast as he could.
  'Brother Dog,' he shouted, 'hide me! The yams are coming.'

'All right,' said Brother Dog. 'Hide behind me but don't say a word.'

So Mr Tiger hid behind Dog.

And down the road came the yams and the noise that their feet made sounded like this:

Ticky picky boom boom
Ticky picky boom boom
Ticky picky boom boom bouf!

The yams said, 'Brother Dog, have you seen Mr Tiger?'

And Brother Dog looked straight ahead and said, 'I can't see Mr Tiger anywhere, not at all.'

But Mr Tiger was so frightened that he called out, 'Don't tell them Brother Dog!' and Dog was so cross that he ran off and left Mr Tiger to the yams.

And the yams jumped.
And Tiger jumped.
And the yams ran.
And Tiger ran.
And the yams galloped.
And Tiger galloped.

Then Mr Tiger saw Sister Duck and all her little ducklings, so he hurried up to her and said, 'Sister Duck, hide me! The yams are coming!'

'All right,' said Sister Duck. 'Get behind me but don't say a word.'

So Mr Tiger hid behind Sister Duck. And down the road came the yams, and the noise that their feet made sounded like this:

Ticky picky boom boom
Ticky picky boom boom
Ticky picky boom boom bouf!

The yams said, 'Sister Duck, have you seen Mr Tiger?'

And Sister Duck looked straight ahead and said, 'Well now, I can't see him anywhere. Nowhere at all.'

But Mr Tiger was so frightened he shouted out, 'Don't tell them Sister Duck,' and Sister Duck was so cross that she moved away and left him to the yams.

And the yams jumped.
And Tiger jumped.
And the yams ran.
And Tiger ran.
And the yams galloped.
And Tiger galloped.

He galloped and galloped, but he was getting tired, and still he could hear the yams coming along the road behind him, getting nearer and nearer. At last, he came to a stream and over the stream was a little plank bridge. On the other side was Mr Goat.

Mr Tiger ran across the bridge and called out, 'Mr Goat, hide me! The yams are coming!'

'All right,' said Mr Goat, 'but don't say a word.'

So Mr Tiger hid behind Mr Goat.

And down the road came the yams,

and the noise that their feet made sounded like this:

    Ticky picky boom boom
    Ticky picky boom boom
    Ticky picky boom boom bouf!

When they reached the bridge, they called out, 'Mr Goat, have you seen Mr Tiger?'

And Mr Goat looked straight ahead but before he could say anything, Mr Tiger shouted, 'Don't tell them, Mr Goat, don't tell them.'

The yams jumped on to the bridge but so did Mr Goat, and he just put down his head and butted them into the stream. Then Mr Goat and Mr Tiger picked the pieces out of the water and took them home to make a great feast of yams. But they certainly did *not* invite Ananse to the feast.

When the nights are dark, Mr Tiger stays at home. He dare not walk along the road, for behind him, he still thinks he hears a noise which sounds like this:

Ticky picky boom boom
Ticky picky boom boom
Ticky picky boom boom bouf!

This is an Ananse story told by Pat Thomson.

Author's Note

The stories about Ananse the trickster spider come from the West Indies and Africa. This particular one comes from Jamaica.

The Happy Lion

There was once a very happy lion. His home was not the hot and dangerous plains of Africa where hunters lie in wait with their guns; it was a lovely French town with brown tile roofs and grey shutters. The happy lion had a house in the town zoo, all for himself, with a large rock garden surrounded by a moat, in the middle of a park with flower beds and a bandstand.

Early every morning, François, the keeper's son, stopped on his way to school to say, *'Bonjour*, Happy Lion.'

In the afternoons, Monsieur Dupont,

the schoolmaster, stopped on his way home to say, '*Bonjour*, Happy Lion.'

In the evenings, Madame Pinson, who knitted all day on the bench by the bandstand, never left without saying, '*Au revoir*, Happy Lion.'

On summer Sundays, the town band filed into the bandstand to play waltzes and polkas. And the happy lion closed his eyes to listen. He loved music. Everyone was his friend and came to say '*Bonjour*' and offer meat and other titbits.

He *was* a happy lion.

One morning, the happy lion found that his keeper had forgotten to close the door of his house.

'Hmm,' he said, 'I don't like that. Anyone may walk in.'

'Oh well,' he added on second thought, 'maybe I will walk out myself and see my friends in town. It will be nice to return their visits.'

So the happy lion walked out into the park and said, '*Bonjour*, my friends' to the busy sparrows.

'*Bonjour*, Happy Lion,' answered the busy sparrows.

And he said, '*Bonjour*, my friend' to the quick red squirrel who sat on his tail and bit into a walnut.

'*Bonjour*, Happy Lion,' said the red squirrel, hardly looking up.

Then the happy lion went into the cobblestone street where he met Monsieur Dupont just around the corner.

'*Bonjour*,' he said, nodding in his polite lion way.

'Hoooooooooohhh . . .' answered Monsieur Dupont, and fainted on to the pavement.

'What a silly way to say *bonjour*,' said the happy lion, and he padded along on his big soft paws.

'*Bonjour*, Mesdames,' the happy lion

said farther down the street when he saw three ladies he had known at the zoo.

'Huuuuuuuuuuuuhhhhhh . . .' cried the three ladies, and ran away as if an ogre were after them.

'I can't think,' said the happy lion, 'what makes them do that. They are always so polite at the zoo.'

'*Bonjour*, Madame.' The happy lion nodded again when he caught up with Madame Pinson near the greengrocer's.

'Oo la la . . . !' cried Madame Pinson, and threw her shopping bag full of vegetables into the lion's face.

'A-a-a-a-choooooo,' sneezed the lion. 'People in this town are foolish, as I begin to see.'

Now the lion began to hear the joyous sounds of a military march. He turned around the next corner, and there was the town band, marching down the street between two lines of people. Ratatatum ratata ratatatum ratatata boom boom.

Before the lion could even nod and say, '*Bonjour*', the music became screams and yells. What a hubbub! Musicians and spectators tumbled into one another in their flight toward doorways and pavement cafes. Soon the street was empty and silent.

The lion sat down and meditated.

'I suppose,' he said, 'this must be the way people behave when they are not at the zoo.'

Then he got up and went on with his stroll in search of a friend who would not faint, or scream, or run away. But the only people he saw were pointing at him excitedly from the highest windows and balconies.

Now what was this new noise the lion heard?

'Toootooooot . . . hoootooo-ooot ooooot . . .' went that noise.

'Hooooot toooooo TOOOOOOOOOHHHOOOOT . . .' and it grew more and more noisy.

'It may be the wind,' said the lion. 'Unless it is the monkeys from the zoo, all of them taking a stroll.'

All of a sudden a big red fire engine burst out of a side street, and came to a stop not too, too far from the lion. Then a big van came backing up on the other side of him with its back door wide open.

The lion just sat down very quietly, for he did not want to miss what was going to happen.

The firemen got off the fire engine and advanced very very slowly toward the lion, pulling their big fire hose along. Very slowly they came closer . . . and closer . . . and the fire hose crawled on like a long snake, longer and longer . . .

SUDDENLY, behind the lion, a little voice cried, *'Bonjour*, Happy Lion.' It was François, the keeper's son, on his way home from school! He had seen the lion and had come running to him. The happy lion was so VERY HAPPY to meet a friend who did not run and who said *'Bonjour'* that he forgot all about the firemen.

And he never found out what they were going to do, because François put his hand on the lion's great mane and said, 'Let's walk back to the park together.'

'Yes, let's,' purred the happy lion.

So François and the happy lion walked back to the zoo. The firemen followed behind in the fire engine, and the people on the balconies and in the high windows shouted at last, *'*BONJOUR! HAPPY LION!'

From then on the happy lion got the best titbits the town saved for him. But if you opened his door he would not wish to go out visiting again. He was happier to sit in his rock garden while on the other side of the moat Monsieur Dupont, Madame Pinson, and all his old friends came again like polite and sensible people to say *'Bonjour*, Happy

Lion.' But he was happiest when he saw François walk through the park every afternoon on his way home from school. Then he swished his tail for joy, for François remained always his dearest friend.

This story is by Louise Fatio.

The Girl and the Geese

Once upon a time, an old man and his wife had a daughter and a son. And the mother said to the daughter, 'Your father and I are off to market. While we are away, be very careful. Look after your little brother; and don't, whatever you do, go out of the house.'

'Yes, mother,' said the girl. But as soon as the old man and his wife were gone to market, she forgot what she had been told, and she left her brother sitting on the doorstep, while she went out to play hopscotch in the street.

And while she was playing hopscotch, a flock of wild geese came down out of the sky, and lifted the little boy on to their wings and flew away with him.

The girl saw the geese, and she ran after them, but they went into a dark wood.

The girl ran to the wood; and she saw a stove. And she said:

'Stove, stove!
Tell! Tell!
Where have the geese gone?'

And the stove said, 'Eat the burnt cake that is in my oven, and I'll tell you where the geese have gone.'

But the girl wouldn't;
so the stove didn't;
and the girl ran on.

She came to an apple tree; and she said:

'Tree, tree!
Tell! Tell!
Where have the geese gone?'

And the tree said, 'Eat the green apple that is on my branch, and I'll tell you where the geese have gone.'

But the girl wouldn't;
so the tree didn't;
and the girl ran on.

She came to a brook of milk with banks of pies; and she said:

'Brook, brook!
Tell! Tell!
Where have the geese gone?'

And the brook said, 'Drink my sour milk and eat my sad pies, and I'll tell you where the geese have gone.'

But the girl wouldn't;
so the brook didn't;
and the girl ran on.

The Girl and the Geese

She met a pig in the wood; and she said:

'Pig, pig!
Tell! Tell!
Where have the geese gone?'

'Into my sty,' said the pig, 'and thrown me out, they have! That's where the geese have gone!'

The girl ran till she came to the sty in the middle of the wood. And there was her little brother, sitting on the floor, and he was playing with apples of gold. She crept into the sty, picked him up in her arms, and ran out again.

But her little brother dropped the golden apples, and he began to cry; and the geese heard him and came flying to catch him again.

The girl ran to the brook of milk; and she said:

'Brook! Brook!
Hide me!
So the wild geese won't find me!'

And the brook said, 'Drink my sour milk, and eat my sad pies.'

And so the girl did;
and so the brook hid;
and the wild geese flew by.

The girl ran on, and soon she heard the geese coming after; and she ran to the apple tree, and she said:

'Tree! Tree!
Hide me!
So the wild geese won't find me!'

And the tree said, 'Eat my green apple.'

And so the girl did;
and so the tree hid;
and the wild geese flew by.

The girl ran on, and soon she heard the geese coming after her; and she ran to the stove, and she said:

'Stove! Stove!
Hide me!
So the wild geese won't find me!'

And the stove said, 'Eat my burnt cake.'

And so the girl did;
and so the stove hid;
and the wild geese flew by.

The girl ran on; she ran out of the wood, and all the way home.

And a good job, too! For here come the old man and his wife, riding back from market!

This story is by Alan Garner.

The Sing-Song of Old Man Kangaroo

Not always was the Kangaroo as now we do behold him, but a Different Animal with four short legs. He was grey and he was woolly, and his pride was inordinate: he danced on an outcrop in the middle of Australia, and he went to the Little God Nqa.

He went to Nqa at six before breakfast, saying, 'Make me different from all other animals by five this afternoon.'

Up jumped Nqa from his seat on the sand-flat and shouted, 'Go away!'

He was grey and he was woolly, and his pride was inordinate: he danced on a rock-ledge in the middle of Australia, and he went to the Middle God Nquing.

He went to Nquing at eight after breakfast, saying, 'Make me different from all other animals; make me, also, wonderfully popular by five this afternoon.'

Up jumped Nquing from his burrow in the spinifex and shouted, 'Go away!'

He was grey and he was woolly, and his pride was inordinate: he danced on a sandbank in the middle of Australia, and he went to the Big God Nqong.

He went to Nqong at ten before dinner-time, saying, 'Make me different from all other animals; make me popular and wonderfully run after by five this afternoon.'

Up jumped Nqong from his bath in the saltpan and shouted, 'Yes, I will!'

Nqong called Dingo – Yellow-Dog Dingo – always hungry, dusty in the sunshine, and showed him Kangaroo. Nqong said, 'Dingo! Wake up, Dingo! Do you see that gentleman dancing on an ashpit? He wants to be popular and very truly run after. Dingo, make him so!'

Up jumped Dingo – Yellow-Dog Dingo – and said, 'What, *that* cat-rabbit?'

Off ran Dingo – Yellow-Dog Dingo – always hungry, grinning like a coal-scuttle – ran after Kangaroo.

Off went the proud Kangaroo on his four little legs like a bunny.

This, O Beloved of mine, ends the first part of the tale!

He ran through the desert; he ran through the mountains; he ran through the salt-pans; he ran through the reed-beds; he ran through the blue gums; he ran through the spinifex; he ran till his front legs ached.

He had to!

Still ran Dingo – Yellow-Dog Dingo – always hungry, grinning like a rat-trap, never getting nearer, never getting farther – ran after Kangaroo.

He had to!

Still ran Kangaroo – Old Man Kangaroo. He ran through the ti-trees; he ran through the mulga; he ran through the long grass; he ran through the short grass; he ran through the Tropics of Capricorn and Cancer; he ran till his hind legs ached.

He had to!

Still ran Dingo – Yellow-Dog Dingo – hungrier and hungrier, grinning like a horse-collar, never getting nearer, never getting farther; and they came to the Wollgong River.

Now, there wasn't any bridge, and there wasn't any ferry-boat, and Kangaroo didn't know how to get over; so he stood on his legs and hopped.

He had to!

He hopped through the Flinders; he hopped through the Cinders; he hopped through the deserts in the middle of Australia. He hopped like a Kangaroo.

First he hopped one yard; then he hopped three yards; then he hopped five yards; his legs growing stronger; his legs growing longer. He hadn't any time for rest or refreshment, and he wanted them very much.

Still ran Dingo – Yellow-Dog Dingo – very much bewildered, very much hungry, and wondering what in the world or out of it made Old Man Kangaroo hop.

For he hopped like a cricket; like a pea in a saucepan; or a new rubber ball on a nursery floor.

He had to!

He tucked up his front legs; he hopped on his hind legs; he stuck out his tail for a balance-weight behind him; and he hopped through the Darling Downs.

He had to!

Still ran Dingo – Tired-Dog Dingo – hungrier and hungrier, very much bewildered, and wondering when in the world or out of it would Old Man Kangaroo stop.

Then came Nqong from his bath in the salt-pan, and said, 'It's five o'clock.'

Down sat Dingo – Poor-Dog Dingo – always hungry, dusty in the sunshine; hung out his tongue and howled.

Down sat Kangaroo – Old Man Kangaroo – stuck out his tail like a milking-stool behind him, and said, 'Thank goodness *that*'s finished!'

Then said Nqong, who is always a gentleman, 'Why aren't you grateful to Yellow-Dog Dingo? Why don't you thank him for all he has done for you?'

Then said Kangaroo – Tired Old Kangaroo – 'He's chased me out of the homes of my childhood; he's chased me out of my regular meal-times; he's altered my shape so I'll never get it back; and he's played Old Scratch with my legs.'

Then said Nqong, 'Perhaps I'm mistaken, but didn't you ask me to make you different from all other animals, as well as to make you very truly sought after? And now it is five o'clock.'

'Yes,' said Kangaroo. 'I wish that I hadn't. I thought you would do it by charms and incantations, but this is a practical joke.'

'Joke!' said Nqong, from his bath in the blue gums. 'Say that again and I'll whistle up Dingo and run your hind legs off.'

'No,' said the Kangaroo. 'I must apologize. Legs are legs, and you needn't alter 'em so far as I am concerned. I only meant to explain to

Your Lordliness that I've had nothing to eat since morning, and I'm very empty indeed.'

'Yes,' said Dingo – Yellow-Dog Dingo – 'I am just in the same situation. I've made him different from all other animals; but what may I have for my tea?'

Then said Nqong from his bath in the salt-pan, 'Come and ask me about it tomorrow, because I'm going to wash.'

So they were left in the middle of Australia, Old Man Kangaroo and Yellow-Dog Dingo, and each said, 'That's *your* fault.'

This is the mouth-filling song
Of the race that was run by a Boomer,
Run in a single burst – only event
  of its kind –
Started by Big God Nqong from
  Warrigaborrigarooma,
Old Man Kangaroo first: Yellow-
  Dog Dingo behind.

Kangaroo bounded away,
His back-legs working like pistons –
Bounded from morning till dark,
Twenty-five feet to a bound.
Yellow-Dog Dingo lay
Like a yellow cloud in the distance –
Much too busy to bark.
My! but they covered the ground!

The Sing-Song of Old Man Kangaroo

Nobody knows where they went,
Or followed the track that they flew in,
For that Continent
Hadn't been given a name.
They ran thirty degrees,
From Torres Straits to the Leeuwin
(Look at the Atlas, please),
And they ran back as they came.

S'posing you could trot
From Adelaide to the Pacific,
For an afternoon's run –
Half what these gentlemen did –
You would feel rather hot,
But your legs would develop terrific –
Yes, my importunate son,
You'd be a Marvellous Kid!

This story is by Rudyard Kipling.

The Naughty Shoes

Have you ever crawled into bed at night with your shoes on? Of course not! You take them off and put them under your chair or under your bed. Grown-ups do the same thing. So just imagine how many thousands of pairs of shoes stand under beds and chairs during the long, dark night, while their owners lie under the covers asleep.

Do the shoes also sleep? Heavens no! Shoes never get tired. Listen to this:

One night my father's left shoe said to my father's right shoe, 'I am sick and tired of taking Father places; all day long I have to go where he wants to go – this way and that way, up way and down way, in way and out way! Now I am going by myself, and I am going the *other* way!'

'I am going with you,' said my father's right shoe.

So off they went through the open window, out into the dark street. It sounded like a man walking in the street, but it was only an empty pair of shoes, going the other way.

'Coming along?' they called through the open window to the neighbours' shoes. And the shoes of the neighbours – husband and wife – joined my father's shoes; their neighbours' shoes came along too, and the shoes of the neighbours of the neighbours, all down the block.

It became quite a parade. Clickety-click went the high heels; boom-boom went the heavy boots; schwee-schwee went the rubbers. Shoes, shoes, and more shoes – old pairs, new pairs, worn-out pairs; shiny shoes, unpolished shoes, scuffed shoes; brown ones, black ones, big ones, small ones. They walked, they ran, they skipped – always the other way, for this was the Free Shoe Parade and their owners' feet were all at home under the covers.

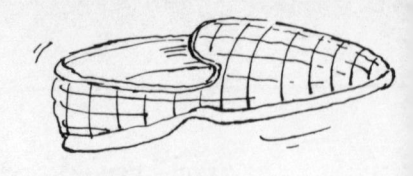

'Left belongs to right!' called the shoes. 'Hold on to each other by the laces!'

But Grandma's left shoe lost track of Grandma's right shoe. And the shoes without laces couldn't hold on to each other at all.

'Where are you? Where are you?' voices called in the dark.

'I'm here! I'm here!' came the answers from here and there and everywhere.

But which belonged to which? There was too much confusion for the right shoes to find their lefts and for the left shoes to find their rights.

'Never mind,' someone shouted. 'Every shoe for himself from now on. We don't need to be paired off.'

And off they went again. Single left shoes and unmatched right shoes. Hoppety-hop. The very dainty and the very shiny shoes waded through all the mud puddles, what fun!

But the old, scuffed shoes, the dirty and unkempt ones, walked primly with neat little steps and avoided the puddles. The shoes of old people hopped, skipped, and jumped. The children's shoes took slow, dignified steps. Shoes without feet cramped inside them. Shoes who were their own masters. They all had a glorious time, a wonderful, marvellous time!

But the fun had to come to an end. The sun came up and shooed away the darkness.

'We have to go home! We have to get back before our people get out of bed!' shouted the shoes, and the jolly parade changed into a scramble of confusion and panic.

Most of the shoes had lost their way and did not know how to get home. As the sun rose higher in the sky, they stampeded through the streets, clickety-click, boom-boom, schwee-

The Naughty Shoes

schwee, scuff-scuff. Boots stomped over slippers. Shoes tripped over their untied laces. Toe-caps banged against toe-caps, and heels stepped on toes.

The sun climbed higher and higher.

'Hurry, hurry!' shouted the shoes. 'We'll be late! Quick, get inside!'

Most of the shoes climbed inside the first open window they saw and settled under the first bed they could find. Two left men's shoes under Grandma's bed. Wading boots under the bed of two-year-old Caroline. And when my father got up, he found under his bed a lady's pump, a blue sneaker, a left slipper, and a right boy's shoe.

'What in the world . . .' said my father.

'What in the world . . .' said all the people in town when they got out of bed. And that morning a parade of limping people went to work and to school, for they were all wearing the wrong shoes. Either too big or too small. Either two right shoes or two left ones – click-scuff, boom-schwee, schwee-click. Grandma went around in stocking feet, and Caroline went barefoot.

Everyone asked, 'Who has my shoes? Who's wearing my shoes?' And everyone examined everyone else's feet. Now and then someone shouted, 'Ah! There's my brown right shoe!' Or, 'Yoo-hoo, you have my red sandal!' And so, slowly but surely, everyone got his own shoes back again.

It took longer for my father, though, than for anyone else. Because his left shoe had climbed a tree, and it was not until three days later that the wind finally blew it down.

This is a Dutch story by Paul Biegel, translated by Celia Amidon.

The House That Grew

Once upon a time there were twin sisters called Mickey and Mouse. They had red hair and blue eyes, and were always ready for adventures.

One day they were in the orchard belonging to their farm. They were lying in the grass kicking their heels when Mickey suddenly stopped picking daisies and said:

'There's a tiny house here. It's no bigger than a mushroom.'

'It looks like stone,' said Mouse, 'but it feels like mushroom. I suppose it has just been hatched and is still soft.'

The house had a steep roof and two chimneys. If the twins laid their cheeks in the grass they could just see a door and windows. As they watched, a ladybird went in at the door.

'I've never seen a ladybird's house before,' said Mickey.

'We knew she had one,' said Mouse, 'because of the nursery rhyme. And she had a lot of children.'

They could not see what was going on inside, but presently the ladybird appeared at the bedroom window. She opened her scarlet wing cases, whirred her wings as if shaking out dust, then closed herself up again and went inside. She did the same out of the second window and then was very busy coming in and out of the door as though collecting things.

'Let's get her some honey,' said the twins, without thinking that there was no way of putting it into such a very small house.

They set off home to get the honey, taking their time about it because it was uphill and quite a long way. When they arrived there were visitors, and so they forgot about the ladybird.

They remembered next morning and hurried to the orchard carrying a pot of honey. They knew exactly where the house had been and could see where they had flattened the grass by lying on it. The house was there, but it had grown twice as big as before. It was now as big as a tea caddy. Mickey poked it with her finger to see if it had hardened. There was an angry buzz from inside and a fat bumble bee in a fur coat pushed its way out of the front door and made some very fierce noises. However, it was too busy for anything but work. It was lining its living room with neat cells for storing honey. Mickey and Mouse poured some on a dock leaf and left it as a peace offering.

When they came down to the orchard on the morning of the third day, the house had grown three times as big as before. Now it was as big as a doll's house, just the right size for a green and blue lizard, who was delighted with it, frisking in and out, sometimes through the door, sometimes through the windows. The twins could see it inside shooting out its tongue to suck the honey out of the cells that the bee had so carefully made. Now and again for a change it thrust its honeyed tongue out of the window and flies came and stuck on it. It ate the flies. When it was too full it lay inside and panted with its eyes shut. The door was still too small for Mouse to get her hand in, or she could have picked it up. But it was quite safe inside, and its house was cool with wet emerald grass waving round it and meadowsweet like elm trees over it.

When Mickey and Mouse went down to the orchard the next day, the house had grown four times as big as before. It was now as big as a suitcase. They could see it as soon as they got to the orchard, and could hear squeals coming from it that seemed to say, 'However long are we going to be left in here alone?' When the twins came near they saw two puppies inside with their paws on the window-sill. The puppies were very pleased to see them. They shot their tongues out of the window to lick Mickey and Mouse and their tails thumped against the walls. 'Let us out, let us out,' they squealed in very high voices. But the door was shut and they were too fat to squeeze through the windows. Mickey and Mouse went to get them some milk. 'We'll bring it every day,' they said.

When they came to the orchard the fifth day, the house had grown five times as big as before. It was as big as a packing crate. The puppies were running loose in the orchard. Mickey and Mouse gave them the milk, then they picked them up and put them in their apron pockets. They had one each, and they called them Pudding and Pie.

In the house there were now two badgers. One was busy filling the larder – one shelf for beetles lying on their backs, one shelf for blackberries and wild strawberries. The other was lining the nursery with clean hay and bracken.

The twins had brought the milk for the puppies in a golden syrup tin and there was still syrup sticking to the sides and bottom. The badgers liked the syrup, but couldn't get their faces far enough into the tin.

'We'll bring them syrup every day,' said the twins, and they went home with their puppies.

But when Mickey and Mouse came down to the orchard on the sixth day, the house was six times as big as before. It was a wonder they could not see it from the farm. The door was big enough for Mickey and Mouse to walk in at. It was open, but they knocked on it, just in case. An answering knock came from inside. They went in rather shyly, and there they found a big-eyed fallow deer. It was eating the badgers'

The House That Grew

nursery hay, tapping with its fore hoof as it ate. It was startled to see strangers, but Mickey and Mouse held out their thumbs dipped in syrup and it sucked them as a calf will, and wagged its tail.

'We will bring some every day,' said the twins.

But when they went down to the orchard the seventh day the house was seven times as big as before. It was as big as a barn and its high stone walls were quite frightening.

'I wonder who lives here now?' said Mickey, as she knocked on the door.

'I DO!' said a horrible Ogre stretching suddenly out of a bedroom window and snatching at them. They dropped their tin of syrup and ran home with all their might. The Ogre ate the syrup, putting his thumb in and sucking it himself.

Mickey and Mouse found their father and mother on the doorstep on the farm pointing very angrily at the house in the orchard.

'Whoever has gone and put a house up in our orchard? It's as big as ours. What impertinence! We'll soon put that where it belongs.'

They rang up the Planning Officer.

The Planning Officer came at once and went to the house in the orchard.

'You've no planning permission for this house,' he said to the Ogre. 'My men are coming tomorrow to knock it down.'

'Sez you,' replied the Ogre, 'but it's YOU who are going to be knocked down.' And he knocked him flat.

Mickey and Mouse said to each other, 'There's only one person stronger than the Ogre. And that's the White Witch.' So they rang up the White Witch.

When the Ogre saw the White Witch at his front door, he ran out at the back screaming like an aeroplane, and was never seen again. Mickey and Mouse had their hands over their ears because of the noise, but they saw that the White Witch was speaking to them.

'This is not just a house like any other,' she said. 'I would say it is distinctly special. I do not think it should be knocked down.'

'We like it better than ours,' said the twins. 'We would like to live in it.'

'Very well,' said the White Witch. 'First I will send my spiders, and afterwards a Very Important Person will come who is Head of All Planners. Now be off home. Come, foggy foggy dew!' She raised her hands and a mist rose up out of the ground and gradually thickened till the twins couldn't see her. They had to run up the hill to keep above the mist that was filling up the valley.

In the morning the mist still hung about with the sun shining through it, but the White Witch's spiders had been there in the night and had covered all the orchard in gossamer. It was wrapped so thickly round everything that you could not tell the house from the trees. When the men from the Planning Office came to knock down the house, they could not see it. They could only see gossamer cartwheels and gossamer nets and gossamer streamers, all sparkling with drops. But the farm house stood clear above the mist on its hill.

'That must be the one we're to knock down,' said the foreman, pointing to the farm. 'It's the only one here so it must be the right one. Bless me! It's still got all the furniture in! Better take that out first.' So they very obligingly took all the furniture out and stacked it in the garden. Then they knocked the farmhouse down and went away very pleased with themselves.

'Whatever will Mummy and Daddy say when they come back from market?' said Mickey and Mouse.

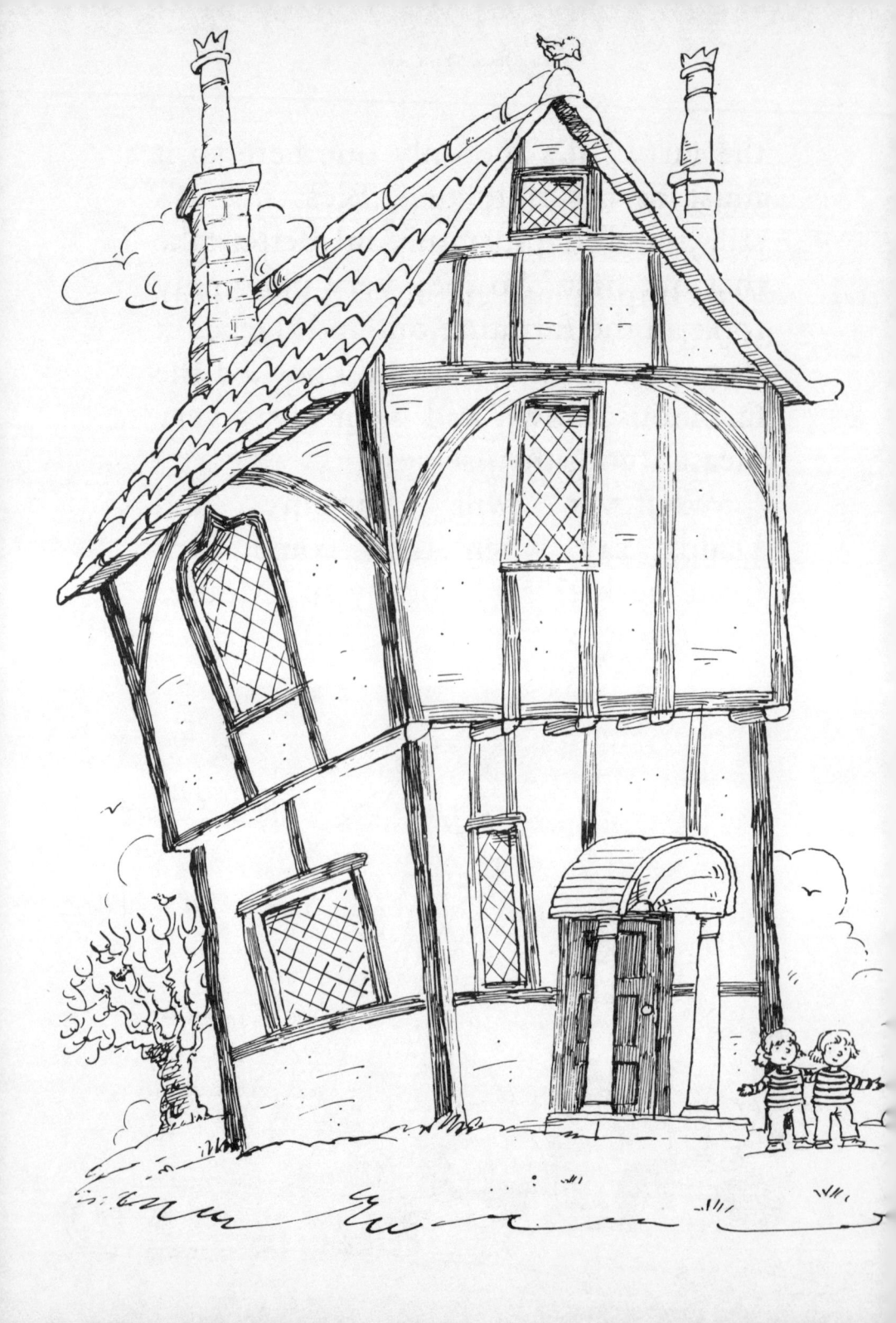

The sun came out warmingly and the breeze blew, till all the gossamer melted away, just in time for the arrival of the Very Important Person who was Head of All Planners. He was followed by a crowd of councillors. They had very clean boots and they held their hats in their hands, but the Very Important Person kept his on. When he saw the house, it was eight times as big as before. It was as big as a castle.

'God bless my soul! I can hardly believe my eyes,' he said. 'I have never seen anything like that in my life. When do you suppose it was built?'

The councillors didn't like to make a guess in case they were wrong, so Mickey and Mouse said:

'Please Sir, it grew.'

The Very Important Person patted the nearest twin on the head.

'Houses don't really grow, young lady,' he said. 'Is the Planner here?'

'No Sir. He is in hospital with a broken jaw.'

'Give him my congratulations for his instant action in removing any building that spoilt the view of this one. And write down this . . .'

The first councillor brought out his note-book.

'Write. "The Old House, Orchard Farm. Name of builder unknown."'

('It grew,' said Mickey and Mouse to each other.)

'Ahem! "Style Native English, earliest known example. To be preserved for all time."'

The Very Important Person then signed it, while all the councillors bowed their heads. Then they all got into their cars and drove away in order of importance. The two least important councillors, while they were waiting for their turn, said to Mickey and Mouse, 'Can we give you a hand to move the furniture in? It's too heavy for you, my dears.'

The twins showed them where they wanted the furniture to go and the men quickly put it all in, with many good-natured jokes.

Mickey and Mouse thanked them warmly.

When their mother and father came back from market, they found they were to live in a great airy house all furnished ready for them and the kettle on the boil. Mickey and Mouse had an attic bedroom where they could look out over the tops of the apple trees. When they went to bed, they said to each other, 'I hope it won't be nine times as big in the morning.'

But the house had finished growing. From the doorway they could see a stall for the deer, a hollow tree for the badger, and a kennel for the puppies. There was a deep crack in the sunniest wall for the lizard. The bee lived in the roof, and the ladybird on a yew bush shaped like a peacock outside the front door.

This story is by Lucy Boston.

The Magic Broom

Phillipippa was the kitchen-maid in King Carraway's palace. She washed the royal dishes, peeled the royal potatoes, and swept the red-tiled floor of the royal kitchen.

She did many other things besides these, but it would take far too long to write them all down here.

One morning the cook sent her to market to buy a new broom.

'That old one is a perfect disgrace to the royal household; you must have a new one at once,' said she crossly.

'Yes, Ma'am,' replied Phillipippa; 'I'll go at once.'

She always said Ma'am when speaking to the cook, as it helped to keep her in a good temper. Phillipippa was very tactful.

The cook was fat. Her cotton print dresses were so tight that they looked as if the buttons might burst at any moment. Phillipippa felt quite nervous about it sometimes.

It didn't take her very long to get to the market-place. She tried several stalls, but couldn't buy a broom anywhere. They had all sold out. Phillipippa stood in the middle of the market square and debated what to do. She dare not go back to the royal palace without a broom. It was very awkward indeed.

Just at that moment along came a pedlar, and under his arm was the most beautiful broom Phillipippa had ever set eyes upon!

'Oh! what a love!' she exclaimed. 'Please, is it for sale?'

'Yes,' said the pedlar. He didn't tell her that he had picked it up in the road that very morning!

Phillipippa bought the broom and hurried back to the royal palace as fast as she could go.

'My word! what a time you've been!' said the cook.

'Indeed, Ma'am, I—'

'That is quite enough from you, Miss, thank you. And don't stand there staring either; anybody would think we had nothing to do. Come and sweep up the kitchen at once! I've been making the stuffing for the royal goose, and the crumbs have gone all over the floor.' The cook snatched up an oven-cloth and banged a saucepan down on the fire with a bump, so that the coals scattered in all directions!

'My! *what* a temper she's got!' thought Phillipippa.

She picked up her new broom and began sweeping the floor. Over the red tiles flew the broom, swish, swish! She had no sooner begun than she had finished! Phillipippa stared in amazement. What a wonderful broom it was! So light! She had never swept the kitchen floor as quickly as *that* before! It must be enchanted!

The Magic Broom

'Well, if that isn't luck!' thought Phillipippa. 'We're going to be great friends, I can see,' she said, patting the broom handle affectionately.

Next day, quite early, a little old woman came knocking at the kitchen door.

Phillipippa was sweeping round the royal larder. She unfastened the door.

'Good morning to you, Miss,' said the little old woman. 'May I ask what you are doing with my broom?'

'*Your* broom?' cried the astonished Phillipippa. 'Why, I bought it myself in the market yesterday.'

'So you may have,' replied the old woman angrily, 'but I tell you it's *my* broom, just the same.'

'Well, and what about me?' the broom asked suddenly in a little, high, squeaky voice.

Phillipippa was so surprised that she let go the broom handle with a jerk.

It didn't fall over, but stood up all by itself in the middle of the floor!

'Come home *at once*,' cackled the witch. 'How *dare* you run away like that!'

'You run away yourself,' piped the broom; 'you horrid old woman! I'm quite happy where I am, thank you.'

'Oh, are you?' cried the witch. 'We'll soon see who is the master here!'

'Oh, shall we?' retorted the broom, and it shook all over with rage. 'Go away at once,' it squeaked, 'or I'll sweep you out!'

'I don't think I should do that,' said Phillipippa, beginning to feel quite alarmed.

But she had no sooner spoken, than the broom began sweeping as hard as it could go. Out of the royal kitchen it swept the old woman, and across the courtyard, so that she had to pick up her petticoats and run. Swish, swish, swish!

Over the drawbridge ran the witch, with the broom close at her heels.

And then, all of a sudden, the broom was back again in Phillipippa's hand, just as if nothing at all had happened! And as for the little old woman, she was nowhere to be seen!

'Well, if that isn't strange!' thought Phillipippa. But she never said one word about it to anybody.

This is an anonymous story from a collection by Barbara Ireson.

Teddy Robinson and the China Gnome

One day Teddy Robinson and Deborah were looking at the marigolds and radishes coming up in their garden when the postman came by with a big parcel for Deborah. On one side it had a label which said FRAGILE. HANDLE WITH CARE.

'Now, what can that be?' said Deborah, and she ran indoors with it and sat Teddy Robinson down on the table so that he could watch while she opened it.

'Fragile. Handle with care,' said Deborah. 'I wonder what it is.'

'It's got a beautiful name,' said Teddy Robinson. 'I wish my name was Fragile, but of course I haven't got a handle.'

'No, it isn't a name,' said Deborah, 'and it doesn't mean it's got a handle. It means it's precious and mustn't be dropped or kicked around in case it gets broken.'

'Ah,' said Teddy Robinson, and he began singing:

> 'Fragile, fragile
> Teddy R.,
> what a precious bear I are.
> Never leave me on the ground
> in case I'm squashed or kicked
>   around.
> Fragile, fragile—'

'Don't be so silly,' said Deborah, 'you aren't fragile. I expect this is some kind of ornament, that's what.'

'Well, I shall be called Fragile too,'

said Teddy Robinson. 'I shall have it for my second name.'

Deborah pulled off the brown paper and opened the box, and there inside, among a lot of straw shavings, she found a china gnome sitting on a china toadstool. He had a bright blue jacket, a pointed red hat, and a long white beard.

'Oh, how sweet!' she said. 'I believe it's an ornament. And there's a letter here too, it says "love from Uncle Michael". I must go and show Mummy.' And off she ran.

'An Ornament,' said Teddy Robinson to himself several times over. 'An Ornament. It sounds rather an important thing to be. More important than Bear or Cat or Dog,' and he began wondering what it was that made an ornament an Ornament, and not just something ordinary.

Deborah came running back.

'Yes,' she said. 'it *is* an ornament. Aren't I lucky? I've had lots of toys, but I've never had an ornament of my own before. I shall keep it here always,' and she put it on the end of the mantelpiece, next to Daddy's pipe-rack.

'But that's where I sit,' said Teddy Robinson.

'Only sometimes,' said Deborah. 'You can sit anywhere because you're a teddy bear. Ornaments have to go on the mantelpiece because they're fragile.'

'Well, that settles it,' said Teddy Robinson. 'I'll be Fragile too. If he sits in my place, then I'll sit in his box. Do you mind lifting me in, very carefully?'

So Deborah lifted him into the box, and Teddy Robinson sat among the straw shavings and felt very precious indeed.

He began singing a little song about it:

'Fragile is my middle name,
handle me with care,
Teddy Fragile Robinson,
the ornamental bear.'

But just then Mummy called to Deborah to bring the box out into the kitchen, because she didn't want the straw shavings all over the carpet. So Teddy Robinson was lifted out again, and that was the last he saw of the box.

He sat on the table and looked up at the china gnome. It wasn't a very friendly looking ornament, but he thought he had better be polite, so he said, 'I hope you're comfortable up there? You get a nice view of everything, being so high up, don't you? I often sit there myself.'

The china gnome didn't even turn his head, but said in a cracked and crusty voice, 'I'm surprised they let you sit up here. The mantelpiece is the place for ornaments, not for toys. I am a very precious and fragile ornament.'

'Well, I'm not exactly a toy,' said Teddy Robinson. 'I am a very precious and fragile teddy bear. I don't wind up or run about on wheels, so you wouldn't exactly call me a toy.'

'Oh, yes, I would,' said the china gnome. 'A soft toy, that's what you are, and you ought to be kept in the toy cupboard. That's the place for soft toys.'

'*Nothing*,' said Teddy Robinson loudly.

'What do you mean?'

'What I say. Deborah's always told me that if I can't think of a polite answer it's better to say nothing. So that's what I said.'

After that he was quiet for a long while because he was thinking all over again about what it was that made an ornament an Ornament, and not just something ordinary.

'Why are you staring at me like that?' said the china gnome.

'I was wondering what it is you've got that I haven't,' said Teddy Robinson.

'You haven't got a beard, or a pointed hat.'

'No, you're right. I wonder I didn't think of it.'

When Deborah came back again Teddy Robinson said, 'Would you be so kind as to make me a pointed hat?'

'Yes, if you like,' said Deborah, and she made him one out of newspaper.

'And now would you get some cotton wool and some string?'

'What ever for?' said Deborah.

'To make me a beard,' said Teddy Robinson.

So Deborah fetched them, and she did just as Teddy Robinson told her, and put a big lump of cotton wool over the lower part of his face, and tied it round his head with a piece of string.

'Now put me on the mantelpiece,' he said, 'and tell me how many ornaments you see there.'

Deborah stood back and looked at the mantelpiece.

'I see the clock,' she said, 'and Daddy's pipe-rack, and one china ornament, and my dear old teddy bear, with cotton wool all over his face and a paper hat on.'

'Oh,' said Teddy Robinson, 'you're quite sure I don't look like an ornament?'

'Quite sure,' said Deborah, laughing. 'You look rather funny, really.'

'All right,' said Teddy Robinson. 'Take them off again. There's no point in making a fool of myself for nothing.'

Deborah had just taken them off again when there was a ring at the doorbell, and a moment later in came Andrew. He admired the china gnome very much, and Deborah told him all about how it had come when she and Teddy Robinson were in the garden.

'And that reminds me,' she said, 'my radishes are nearly ready to be picked. Come and see.'

'I'll just fetch Spotty in,' said Andrew, 'I left him in the hall.'

Spotty was Andrew's toy dog who usually came with him when he came to play with Deborah. Teddy Robinson didn't care for him much because he always wanted to argue, so he quickly put on his Thinking Face and pretended to be making up poetry.

Andrew put them side by side in the armchair.

'They can talk to each other while we're busy,' he said.

When the others had gone the spotted dog stared hard at the gnome with his black boot-button eyes, and said rudely, 'That's new. What is it?'

'It's an ornament,' whispered Teddy Robinson.

'Ah, yes, of course. Very useful things, ornaments,' said the spotted dog, who always knew everything.

'What for?' asked Teddy Robinson.

'For being ornamental, of course,' said Spotty.

'Oh,' said Teddy Robinson. 'Yes, of course. What does ornamental mean, exactly?'

'It's what ornaments are,' said Spotty. 'Surely you knew that?'

'Yes,' said Teddy Robinson. 'Of course. I don't know why I asked.'

'Nor do I,' said Spotty. He then stared hard at the china gnome again and barked rudely, 'Hey, Mister Ornament! How do you like living with a teddy bear who doesn't know what ornamental means?'

The china gnome said, in a sharp, cracked voice, 'I don't like it at all. Neither do I like being shouted at by a rude dog who ought to be outside in a kennel.'

The spotted dog looked very surprised.

'This place seems more like a zoo

than a house,' said the china gnome. 'You ought to be outside in the garden.'

'Oh, no,' said Teddy Robinson, 'Spotty isn't a real dog, he's a real *toy* dog; same as I'm not a real bear, but a real *teddy* bear.'

'Then he ought to go in the toy cupboard too,' said the gnome.

There was a rustling noise at the open window, and the Next Door Kitten jumped up on the sill.

'Hallo,' she purred, when she saw Teddy Robinson in the chair. 'Are you coming out?'

'Not just now,' said Teddy Robinson, 'but won't you come in?'

'Thank you,' said the Next Door Kitten, and she jumped through the window and landed on the arm of the chair.

'Who's the old gentleman on the mantelpiece?' she whispered through her whiskers.

'*That*,' said the spotted dog in a loud, rude voice, 'is the ugliest, nastiest—'

But Teddy Robinson said quickly, 'Sssh! He's an ornament. He's come to live here.'

The Next Door Kitten jumped lightly on to the mantelpiece and picked her way carefully along to the china gnome.

'Miaou do you do?' she said politely. 'What purrr-fectly lovely weather we're having.'

'Get down! Get down at once!' snapped the china gnome. 'How dare you get up here?'

The Next Door Kitten stepped back, surprised.

'But I often come up here,' she said. 'I come to talk to Teddy Robinson when he's sitting up here.'

'Well, he's not going to sit up here any longer,' said the gnome. 'I don't like my sitting-room cluttered up with a lot of soft toys. I'm going to arrange for him to live in the toy cupboard. It isn't as if he were an ornament. As for you, get down at once and go back in the garden where you belong. I won't have wild animals in my room.'

'But it's not your room,' said the Next Door Kitten, 'it's Teddy Robinson's, and he invited me in.'

'Yes, I did!' shouted Teddy Robinson from the armchair, 'but I never invited you. You just came in a parcel without being asked. I've tried to be polite to you and make you feel at home. I've let you sit in my place on the mantelpiece, but all you've done is be rude to me and my friends, so now I'm not going to try to make you feel at home any more. A gnome in the home is a terrible bore, and I don't want a gnome in my home any more. I shall ask Deborah to have you taken away.'

He stopped for breath; then he said, 'If I wasn't so angry I'd make a song about it. I nearly did by mistake.'

Just then they heard footsteps outside. The Next Door Kitten turned quickly, brushing against the china gnome by mistake, and jumped down off the mantelpiece. At the same minute the china gnome fell with a thud on the carpet.

No-one spoke. The Next Door Kitten jumped out of the window, and sat washing her paws quietly on the ledge outside, as if nothing had happened. Then Teddy Robinson peered over the edge of the chair to see what had happened to the china gnome. He was still all in one piece, but there was a long crack down one side of his blue china jacket.

'Poor thing,' said Teddy Robinson kindly, 'I'm afraid you're cracked.'

'Mind your own business,' said the china gnome, and his voice sounded crustier and more cracked than ever. 'I don't talk to soft toys.'

'Well, I may be soft,' said Teddy Robinson, 'but I'm glad I'm not cracked.'

Then the door opened and in came Deborah and Andrew.

'Oh!' said Deborah, 'my ornament has fallen down!'

'And it's cracked down one side,' said Andrew.

'Never mind,' said Mummy, coming

in after them, 'it won't show when he's in the garden where he belongs.'

'In the garden?' said Deborah, surprised.

'Yes,' said Mummy, 'he's a garden ornament. Didn't you read Uncle Michael's letter?'

'Oh, no, I forgot!' said Deborah. 'It was such grown-up writing. But I thought he'd sit on the mantelpiece.'

'Oh, no,' said Mummy, 'I don't think he'd look right in here at all, but he'll be lovely in your garden.'

'Oh, yes! He can look after the plants!' said Deborah.

'And frighten the birds away,' said Teddy Robinson.

'Like a scarecrow,' said the spotted dog.

So the china gnome was taken out and put in Deborah's garden, all among the radishes and marigolds, where he really looked quite pretty. Then

Deborah found Uncle Michael's letter and read it aloud to Teddy Robinson. It said:

Dear Deborah,

I hope you will like this little gnome for your garden. I think his name must be Grumpy because he looks rather cross, so he may be useful for frightening the slugs and earwigs away. I didn't buy you an indoor ornament because of course you have always got Teddy Robinson.

Love from,
UNCLE MICHAEL

'I think that is a very sensible letter,' said Teddy Robinson. 'I always did like Uncle Michael. Can I sit on the mantelpiece again now?'

'Of course,' said Deborah, and she lifted him up.

'There's just one thing more I want to know,' said Teddy Robinson. 'What exactly *is* an ornament?'

'Why, you funny old boy,' said Deborah. 'Surely you knew that? It's something you put on a shelf because it looks pretty.'

'Well, fancy that!' said Teddy Robinson. 'Then I've been an Ornament all along and I never knew.'

And that is the end of the story about Teddy Robinson and the china gnome.

This story is by Joan G. Robinson.

Omumbo-rombonga

Tortoise had a dream. He dreamt of a tree which was in a secret place. From the tree's branches grew all the fruits of the earth – bananas, dates, coconuts, melons, millet, yams, cassava, maize, pineapples and oranges.

Tortoise told the animals about the tree of his dream. 'From its branches grow – bananas, dates, coconuts, melons, millet, yams, cassava, maize, pineapples and oranges.'

The Lion laughed. 'It's only a dream,' he said.

'No,' said Tortoise. 'It is real. I will go to Grandmother Koko. She will know where it grows.'

'You are too slow and steady,' said the Lion. 'I will go myself.'

The Lion went.

He told Grandmother Koko about Tortoise's dream.

'I have heard of this tree,' said Grandmother Koko. 'Its name is Omumbo-rombonga. But if you want the fruit to fall you must call out its name.'

'Omumbo-rombonga,' said the Lion. 'How shall I find the tree?'

'If you remember the name you will find the tree. If you remember the name the fruit will fall,' said Grandmother

Koko. 'But don't look round on your way back or the name will go out of your head.'

The Lion was fierce and he was bold. He wouldn't forget the name.

'Omumbo-rombonga,' he said. But on his way back he looked round . . .

THUD! He tripped over an ant hill. The name went out of his head.

'Omrongbing . . . ?'

Next went the Elephant.

'Mind the ant hill,' said the Lion.

'The name of the tree is Omumbo-rombonga,' said Grandmother Koko. 'And don't look round.'

The Elephant was big and he was strong. He wouldn't forget the name. 'Omumbo-rombonga,' he said. On his way back he saw the ant hill. But then he looked round . . .

OUCH! He trod on a thorn instead. The name went out of his head.

'Bongarombo . . . ?'

Next went the Hyena.

'Mind the thorn,' said the Elephant.

'The name of the tree is Omumbo-rombonga,' said Grandmother Koko. 'And don't look round.'

The Hyena was cunning and she was sly. She wouldn't forget the name.

'Omumbo-rombonga,' she said. She saw the ant hill. She saw the thorn. But then she looked round . . .

SPLASH! She fell into a pool of water. The name went out of her head.

'Bing-bong-bang . . . ?'

Next went the Ostrich.

'Mind the pool,' said the Hyena.

'The name of the tree is Omumbo-rombonga,' said Grandmother Koko. 'And don't look round.'

The Ostrich was fast and he was speedy. He wouldn't forget the name.

'Omumbo-rombonga,' he said. He saw the ant hill. He saw the thorn. He saw the pool. But then he looked round

– HISSS! There was a large snake at his feet. The name went out of his head.

'Mabomba . . . ?'

Next went the Baboon.

'Mind the snake,' said the Ostrich.

'The name of the tree is Omumbo-rombonga,' said Grandmother Koko. 'And don't look round . . .'

The Baboon was clever and he was wise. He wouldn't forget the name.

'Omumbo-rombonga,' he said.

He saw the ant hill. He saw the

thorn. He saw the pool. He saw the snake. But then he looked round . . .

SWISH! He was caught in a creeper. The name went out of his head.

'Mumbo-bumbo . . . ?'

Next went the Giraffe.

'Mind the creeper,' said the Baboon.

'The name of the tree is Omumbo-rombonga,' said Grandmother Koko. 'And don't look round.'

The Giraffe was stately and she was proud. She wouldn't forget the name.

'Omumbo-rombonga,' she said. She saw the ant hill. She saw the thorn. She saw the pool. She saw the snake. She saw the creeper. But then she looked round . . .

SPLAT! She slipped on a patch of mud. The name went out of her head.

'Mim-bim-obo . . . ?'

'Please let me go,' said Tortoise. The animals let him go.

'Mind the mud,' said the Giraffe.

'The name of the tree is Omumbo-rombonga,' said Grandmother Koko. 'And don't look round.'

Tortoise was slow and he was steady. He wouldn't forget the name. 'Omumbo-rombonga,' he said. He saw the ant hill. He saw the thorn. He saw the pool. He saw the snake. He saw the creeper. He saw the mud . . . And he didn't look round. So he saw the scorpion in his path.

'Lucky I didn't look round,' thought Tortoise. 'Omumbo-rombonga,' he said to himself.

'Have you remembered the name?' said the animals, as they saw Tortoise slowly and steadily coming.

'Look behind you,' said Tortoise.

And there was the Omumbo-rombonga tree. From its branches grew bananas, dates, coconuts, melons, millet, yams, cassava, maize, pineapples and oranges.

'Omumbo-rombonga,' cried Tortoise.

Down showered the bananas, the dates, the coconuts, the melons, the millet, the yams, the cassava, the maize, the pineapples and the oranges.

After the animals had eaten, Tortoise said, 'Let everyone plant a seed.'

The seeds grew. So now the animals have food of their own, grown from the fruits of the Omumbo-rombonga tree.

This story is a retelling of the traditional tale by Joanna Troughton.

Author's Note

The story of the miraculous tree, and of Tortoise who remembered its name, comes from the Bantu people of Africa. Many different versions are told in places as far apart as Cameroon in the north and Transvaal in the south.

The Riddle-Me-Ree

*'In marble walls as white as milk,
Lined with a skin as soft as silk,
Within a fountain crystal clear,
A golden apple doth appear.
No doors there are to this stronghold,
Yet thieves break in and steal the gold.'*

Little Tim Rabbit asked this riddle when he came home from school one day.

Mrs Rabbit stood with her paws on her hips, admiring her young son's cleverness.

'It's a fine piece of poetry,' said she.

'It's a riddle,' said Tim. 'It's a riddle-me-ree. Do you know the answer, Mother?'

'No, Tim,' Mrs Rabbit shook her head. 'I'm not good at riddles. We'll ask your father when he comes home. I can hear him stamping his foot outside. He knows everything, does Father.'

Mr Rabbit came bustling in. He flung down his bag of green food, mopped his forehead, and gave a deep sigh.

'There! I've collected enough for a family of elephants. I got lettuces, carrots, wild thyme, primrose leaves and tender shoots. I hope you'll make a good salad, Mother.'

'Can you guess a riddle?' asked Tim.

'I hope so, my son. I used to be very good at riddles. What is a Welsh Rabbit? Cheese! Ha ha!'

'Say it again, Tim,' urged Mrs

Rabbit. 'It's such a good piece of poetry, and all.'

So Tim Rabbit stood up, put his hands behind his back, tilted his little nose and stared at the ceiling. Then in a high squeak he recited his new riddle:

'In marble walls as white as milk,
Lined with a skin as soft as silk,
Within a fountain crystal clear,
A golden apple doth appear.
No doors there are to this stronghold,
Yet thieves break in and steal the gold.'

Father Rabbit scratched his head, and frowned.

'Marble walls,' said he. 'Hum! Ha! That's a palace. A golden apple. No doors. I can't guess it. Who asked it, Tim?'

'Old Jonathan asked us at school today. He said anyone who could guess it should have a prize. We can hunt and we can holler, we can ask and beg, but we must give him the answer by tomorrow.'

'I'll have a good think, my son,' said Mr Rabbit. 'We mustn't be beaten by a riddle.'

All over the common Father Rabbits were saying, 'I'll have a good think,' but not one Father knew the answer, and all the small bunnies were trying to guess.

Tim Rabbit met Old Man Hedgehog down the lane. The old fellow

The Riddle-Me-Ree

was carrying a basket of crab-apples for his youngest daughter. On his head he wore a round hat made from a cabbage leaf. Old Man Hedgehog was rather deaf, and Tim had to shout.

'Old Man Hedgehog. Can you guess a riddle?' shouted Tim.

'Eh?' The Hedgehog put his hand up to his ear. 'Eh?'

'A riddle!' cried Tim.

'Aye. I knows a riddle,' said Old Hedgehog. He put down his basket and lighted his pipe. 'Why does a Hedgehog cross a road? Eh? Why, for to get to t'other side.' Old Hedgehog laughed wheezily.

'Do you know this one?' shouted Tim.

'Which one? Eh?'

'In marble walls as white as milk,' said Tim, loudly.

'I could do with a drop of milk,' said Hedgehog.

'Lined with a skin as soft as silk,' shouted Tim.

'Nay, my skin isn't like silk. It's prickly, is a Hedgehog's skin,' said the Old Hedgehog.

'Within a fountain crystal clear,' yelled Tim.

'Yes. I knows it. Down the field. There's a spring of water, clear as crystal. Yes, that's it,' cried Old Hedgehog, leaping about in excitement. 'That's the answer, a spring.'

'A golden apple doth appear,' said Tim, doggedly.

'A gowd apple? Where? Where?' asked Old Hedgehog, grabbing Tim's arm.

'No doors there are to this stronghold,' said Tim, and now his voice was getting hoarse.

'No doors? How do you get in?' cried the Hedgehog.

'Yet thieves break in and steal the

The Riddle-Me-Ree

gold.' Tim's throat was sore with shouting. He panted with relief.

'Thieves? That's the Fox again. Yes. That's the answer.'

'No. It isn't the answer,' said Tim, patiently.

'I can't guess a riddle like that. Too long. No sense in it,' said Old Man Hedgehog at last. 'I can't guess 'un. Now here's a riddle for you. It's my own, as one might say. My own!'

'What riddle is that?' asked Tim.

'Needles and Pins, Needles and Pins,
When Hedgehog marries his trouble
  begins.'

'What's the answer? I give it up,' said Tim.

'Why, Hedgehog. Needles and Pins, that's me.' Old Man Hedgehog threw back his head and stamped his feet and roared with laughter, and little Tim

125

laughed too. They laughed and they laughed.

'Needles and Pins. Darning needles and hair pins,' said Old Hedgehog.

There was a rustle behind them, and they both sprang round, for Old Hedgehog could smell even if he was hard of hearing.

Out of the bushes poked a sharp nose, and a pair of bright eyes glinted through the leaves. A queer musky smell filled the air.

'I'll be moving on,' said Old Man Hedgehog. 'You'd best be getting along home too, Tim Rabbit. Your mother wants you. Good day. Good day.'

Old Hedgehog trotted away, but the Fox stepped out and spoke in a polite kind of way.

'Excuse me,' said he. 'I heard merry laughter and I'm feeling rather blue. I should like a good laugh. What's the joke?'

The Riddle-Me-Ree

'Old Man Hedgehog said he was needles and pins,' stammered poor little Tim Rabbit, edging away.

'Yes. Darning needles and hair pins,' said the Fox. 'Why?'

'It was a riddle,' said Tim.

'What about riddles?' asked the Fox.

'Marble milk, skin silk
Fountain clear, apple appear.
No doors. Thieves gold,'

Tim gabbled.

'Nonsense. Rubbish,' said the Fox. 'It isn't sense. I know a much better riddle.'

'What is it, sir?' asked Tim, forgetting his fright.

'Who is the fine gentleman in the red jacket who leads the hunt?' asked the Fox, with his head aside.

'I can't guess at all,' said Tim.

'A Fox. A Fox of course. He's the finest gentleman at the hunt.' He laughed so much at his own riddle that little Tim Rabbit had time to escape down the lane and to get home to his mother.

'Well, has anyone guessed the riddle?' asked Mrs Rabbit.

'Not yet, Mother, but I'm getting on,' said Tim.

Out he went again in the opposite direction, and he met the Mole.

'Can you guess a riddle, Mole?' he asked.

'Of course I can,' answered the Mole. 'Here it is:

> A little black man in a hole,
> Pray tell me if he is a Mole,
> If he's dressed in black velvet,
> He's Moldy Warp Delvet,
> He's a Mole, up a pole, in a hole.'

'I didn't mean that riddle,' said Tim. 'I haven't time for anybody else's

The Riddle-Me-Ree

riddles,' said the Mole, and in a flurry of soil he disappeared into the earth.

'He never stopped to listen to my recitation,' said Tim sadly.

He ran on, over the fields. There were Butterflies to hear his riddle, and Bumble-bees and Frogs, but they didn't know the answer. They all had funny little riddles of their own and nobody could help Tim Rabbit. So on he went across the wheatfield, right up to the farmyard, and he put his nose under the gate. That was as far as he dare go.

'Hallo, Tim Rabbit,' said the Cock. 'What do you want today?'

'Pray tell me the answer to a riddle,' said Tim politely. 'I've brought a pocketful of corn for a present. I gathered it in the cornfield on the way.'

The Cock called the Hens to listen to Tim's riddle. They came in a crowd, clustering round the gate, chattering loudly. Tim Rabbit settled himself on a stone so that they could see him. He wasn't very big, and there were many of them, clucking and whispering and shuffling their feet and shaking their feathers.

'Silence!' cried the Cock. 'Silence for Tim Rabbit.'

The Hens stopped shuffling and lifted their heads to listen.

Once more Tim recited his poem, and once more here it is:

'In marble walls as white as milk,
Lined with a skin as soft as silk,
Within a fountain crystal clear,
A golden apple doth appear.
No doors there are to this stronghold,
Yet thieves break in and steal the gold.'

There was silence for a moment as Tim finished, and then such a rustle and murmur and tittering began, and the Hens put their little beaks together, and chortled and fluttered their wings and laughed in their sleeves.

'We know! We know!' they clucked.

'What is it?' asked Tim.

'An egg,' they all shouted together, and their voices were so shrill the farmer's wife came to the door to see what was the matter.

So Tim threw the corn among them, and thanked them for their cleverness.

'And here's a white egg to take home with you, Tim,' said the prettiest hen, and she laid an egg at Tim's feet.

How joyfully Tim ran home with the answer to the riddle! How gleefully he put the egg on the table!

'Well, have you guessed it?' asked Mrs Rabbit.

'It's there! An egg,' nodded Tim, and they all laughed and said: 'Well, I never! Well, I never thought of that!'

And the prize from Old Jonathan, when Tim gave the answer? It was a little wooden egg, painted blue, and when Tim opened it, there lay a tiny carved hen with feathers of gold.

This story is by Alison Uttley.

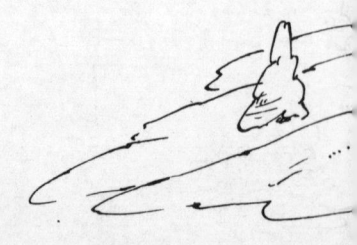

The Tomten

It is the dead of night. The old farm lies fast asleep and everyone inside the house is sleeping too.

The farm is deep in the middle of the forest. Once upon a time someone came here, cut down trees, built a homestead and farmed the land. No-one knows who. The stars are shining in the sky tonight, the snow lies white all around, the frost is cruel. On such a night people creep into their small houses, wrap themselves up and bank the fire on the hearth.

Here is a lonely old farm where everyone is sleeping. All but one . . .

The Tomten is awake. He lives in a corner of the hayloft and comes out at night when human beings are asleep. He is an old, old tomten who has seen the snow of many hundreds of winters. No-one knows when he came to the farm. No-one has ever seen him, but they know he is there. Sometimes when they wake up they see the prints of his feet in the snow. But no-one has seen the Tomten.

On small silent feet the Tomten moves about in the moonlight. He peeps into cowshed and stable, storehouse and toolshed. He goes between the buildings making tracks in the snow.

The Tomten goes first to the cowshed. The cows are dreaming that summer is here, and they are grazing in the fields. The Tomten talks to them in tomten language, a silent little language the cows can understand.

*'Winters come and winters go,
Summers come and summers go,
Soon you can graze in the fields.'*

The moon is shining into the stable. There stands Dobbin, thinking. Perhaps he remembers a clover field, where he trotted around last summer. The Tomten talks to him in tomten language, a silent little language a horse can understand.

> '*Winters come and winters go,*
> *Summers come and summers go,*
> *Soon you will be in your clover*
>   *field.*'

Now all the sheep and lambs are sleeping soundly. But they bleat softly when the Tomten peeps in at the door. He talks to them in tomten language, a silent little language the sheep can understand.

> '*All my sheep, all my lambs,*
> *The night is cold, but your wool is warm,*
> *And you have aspen leaves to eat.*'

Then on small silent feet the Tomten goes to the chicken house, and the chickens cluck contentedly when he comes. He talks to them in tomten language, a silent little language chickens can understand.

'Lay me an egg, my jolly chickens, and I will give you corn to eat.'

The dog kennel roof is white with snow, and inside is Caro. Every night he waits for the moment when the Tomten will come. The Tomten is his friend, and he talks to Caro in tomten language, a silent little language a dog can understand.

'Caro, my friend, is it cold tonight? Are you cold in your kennel? I'll fetch more straw and then you can sleep.'

The house where the people live is silent. They are sleeping through the winter night without knowing that the Tomten is there.

> *'Winters come and winters go,*
> *I have seen people large and small*
> *But never have they seen me,'*

thinks the Tomten.

He tiptoes across to the children's cot, and stands looking for a long time.

'If they would only wake up, then I could talk to them in tomten language, a silent little language children can understand. But children sleep at night.'

And away goes the Tomten on his little feet. In the morning the children see his tracks, a line of tiny footprints in the snow.

Then the Tomten goes back to his cosy little corner in the hayloft. There, in the hay, the cat is waiting for him, for she wants milk. The Tomten talks to the cat in tomten language, a silent little language a cat can understand.

'Of course you may stay with me, and of course I will give you milk,' says the Tomten.

Winter is long and dark and cold, and sometimes the Tomten dreams of summer.

'Winters come and winters go,
Summers come and summers go,
Soon the swallows will be here,'

thinks the Tomten.

But the snow still lies in deep drifts around the old farm in the forest. The stars shine in the sky, it is biting cold. On such a night people creep into their small houses and bank the fire on the hearth. Here is a lonely old farm, where everyone is fast asleep. All but one . . .

Winters come and summers go, year

follows year, but as long as people live at the old farm in the forest, every night the Tomten will trip around between the houses on his small silent feet.

This story is by Astrid Lindgren.

Danny Fox Steals Some Fish

Danny Fox lived in a small cave on the side of a mountain near the sea. He had a wife called Doxie and three children who were always hungry. Danny and Doxie were often hungry too. The names of their children were Lick, Chew, and Swallow.

Out on the mountain it was very cold, but in the cave it was warm and snug and Danny Fox liked to sleep curled up, with his nose tucked under his hind leg and his long bushy tail round his face like a scarf. Mrs Doxie Fox liked to sleep curled up, with her nose tucked underneath Lick's chin and her front legs hugging Chew and her hind legs hugging Swallow. And Lick, Chew, and Swallow liked to sleep curled up like furry balls against their mother's tummy, while she covered their backs with her long bushy tail like a scarf.

One day the little foxes woke up early and began to whine and yelp and howl.

'Why are you whining, Lick?' said Mrs Doxie Fox.

'I'm whining because I have nothing to lick,' said Lick to his mother, Mrs Doxie Fox.

'Why are you yelping, Chew?' said Mrs Doxie Fox.

'I'm yelping because I have nothing to chew,' said Chew to his mother.

'Why are you howling, Swallow?' said Mrs Doxie Fox.

'I'm howling because I have nothing to swallow,' said Swallow.

'Oh please stop whining and yelping and howling,' said Mrs Doxie Fox, 'and I'll ask your father to fetch some food. Wake up, Danny Fox. It is time to go hunting.'

'I'm not awake yet,' said Danny Fox, and his voice sounded muffled underneath his bushy tail.

'Then how did you hear what I said?' said Mrs Doxie Fox.

'I heard you in my sleep,' said Danny Fox. 'And now I'm talking in my sleep.' But he opened one eye and they knew he was only pretending. Lick, Chew, and Swallow thought he wasn't going to move, so they began their hullabaloo again.

'Oh please fetch some food,' said Mrs Doxie Fox. 'Lick, Chew, and Swallow need something to lick, chew and swallow, and I need something too.'

Danny Fox sat up and yawned. He stretched out his front legs and yawned and he stretched out his hind legs and yawned. Then he put his nose outside the cave and sniffed the cold air.

'Sniff, sniff. I can sniff a rabbit.' He began to run faster and faster up the mountainside, sniffing the ground. Then he saw the rabbit, and yelped and ran faster than ever. But the rabbit escaped by diving into a crack between two rocks. The crack was too narrow for Danny.

He trotted along and he trotted along. Then suddenly he stood quite still, with his bushy tail stretched out behind him and his long, smooth nose stretched out in front.

'Sniff, sniff. I can sniff a pigeon.' He looked and he looked and he saw a wood-pigeon just below him on the hill, pecking at the ground. He walked very quietly, one step at a time. Then suddenly he sprang at the pigeon. But the pigeon saw him just in time and flew away, and Danny turned head over heels and rolled down the hill.

'Sniff, sniff,' said Danny at the bottom of the hill. 'I can sniff a mouse.' But the mouse ran into its hole.

He trotted along and he trotted along till he came to a farm at the foot of the mountain.

'Sniff, sniff. I can sniff a hen.' But the hen saw him and flew up to a branch of a tree.

'Sniff, sniff. I can sniff a duck.' But the duck waddled into the farmer's house, where Danny was afraid to go.

'Sniff, sniff. I can sniff a goose.' But the goose made such a noise that the farmer came out to see what was wrong and Danny had to hide beneath a bush. 'I am unlucky this morning,' he said to himself. 'What can I find to take home?'

When the farmer had gone, he sneaked out of the farmyard and began to trot along the road. The road went along by the sea-shore, from the harbour to the town.

'Sniff, sniff. That's funny. I can sniff a fish.'

Danny trotted along and he trotted along, feeling very hungry. The smell of fish got stronger and stronger, and the more he smelt it the hungrier he grew. His mouth watered, his pink tongue hung out and saliva dribbled from it on to the road. He sniffed and sniffed and began to run fast. Then he came round a corner and suddenly stopped.

He saw a horse and cart in front of him. The horse was walking very slowly, the driver seemed to be asleep and the cart was loaded with boxes of fish, all gleaming silver.

Danny Fox walked very quietly, one step at a time. Then he ran very quietly with his bushy tail stretched out behind him and his long smooth nose pointing up towards the cart. When he was near enough he sprang on to the cart and grabbed a fish from one of the open boxes. The driver did not look round. Danny Fox lay down very quietly, hoping not to wake him. His plan was to eat one fish, then pick up as many as he could hold in his mouth and jump off the cart and run home with them. He took a little mouthful of fish and the driver did not look round. He took a bigger mouthful of fish and the driver did not look round. Danny Fox watched him for a moment and saw that his hair was black and curly. He looked young and slim and strong.

'What a pity,' thought Danny. 'I wish he was old and slow!' And he lay down very quietly, hoping not to wake him. And crunch, crunch, crunch, he took a great big noisy mouthful and the driver jumped up and brought his whip down – swish! – on the white tip of his tail. Danny Fox leapt off the cart and over a stone wall into a field.

Now he was very unhappy. He had eaten three mouthfuls of fish, but had nothing to bring home to Lick, Chew, and Swallow, and nothing for Doxie either. The cart had gone on but – 'sniff, sniff, sniff' – he could still smell the fish as he lay hiding behind the wall.

He lay and he lay and he thought and he thought, till he thought of a plan. Then he got up quickly and he ran and he ran, keeping close behind the wall so that the driver of the cart could not see him. He ran till he came to a place where the road turned a corner, and by now the cart was far behind him. Then he jumped over the wall and lay down in the middle of the road pretending to be dead.

He lay there a long time. He heard the cart coming nearer and nearer. He kept his eyes shut. He hoped the driver would see him and not run him over.

When the driver saw Danny lying stretched in the middle of the road, he stopped his cart and said, 'That's funny. That's the fox that was stealing my fish. That's the fox I hit with my whip. I thought I had only touched the tip of his tail, but now I see I must have hurt him badly. He must have run away from me ahead of my cart. And now he is dead.' He got down from his cart and stooped to look at Danny.

'What a beautiful red coat he's got,' the driver said, 'and what beautiful, thick red trousers. What a beautiful long bushy tail, with a beautiful white tip. What a beautiful long smooth nose with a beautiful black tip. I'll take him home with me, I think, and skin him and sell his fur.'

So he picked up Danny Fox and threw him on to the cart on top of the boxes of fish. The cart went on. Danny opened one eye and saw the driver's back was turned to him. Then very quietly, he slid the tip of his tail underneath a fish and flicked it on to the road. He lay quite still and threw another fish out with his tail, then another and another and another, till all down the road behind the cart there was a long, long line of fish stretching into the distance. And the driver never looked round because he thought Danny was dead. At the next corner, Danny jumped off the cart and ran back down the road. When the cart was out of sight, he started to pick the fish up.

He picked up one for Lick. He picked up one for Chew. He picked up one for Swallow. He tried to pick up one for Doxie too but his mouth was too full, so off he ran towards home with three fishes' heads sticking out from one side of his mouth and three fishes' tails sticking out from the other.

He ran past the farm, and the duck

Danny Fox Steals Some Fish

and the goose and the hen were watching him.

'Look out,' said the duck. 'There goes Danny Fox!'

'That's funny,' said the goose, 'he has grown new whiskers.'

'Those aren't whiskers,' said the hen.

'Yes they are,' said the goose.

'No, they're not,' said the hen.

'What are they, then?' said the duck.

'They are three fishes' heads on one side of his mouth,' said the hen, 'and three fishes' tails on the other.'

Danny ran along the bottom of the mountain past the mouse's hole. The mouse was peeping out.

'That's funny,' said the mouse. 'I can see three fishes running along. But they have legs like a fox.'

'Fishes don't have legs,' said the pigeon who was flying up above.

'Yes, they do,' said the mouse.

'No, they don't,' said the pigeon.

'These ones do,' said the mouse.

Danny Fox ran up the mountain past the crack in the rocks where the rabbit was hiding.

'That's funny,' said the rabbit. 'Danny Fox has been out fishing. I didn't know he had a boat.'

At last Danny reached home. He threw one fish to Lick, and one fish to Chew and one fish to Swallow and while they were licking and chewing and swallowing he said to their mother, 'Come quickly with me.'

Doxie and Danny Fox ran down the mountain again till they came to the road – and after they had eaten three fish each, they picked up three fish each and carried them home. Then they went back for another three fish each, and another three fish each and another three fish each. They went on all morning carrying fish up the mountain, until there were no more left on the road.

So Danny and Doxie and Lick and Chew and Swallow had an enormous feast. They ate and they ate until they could eat no more. Then they all fell down together in a heap, fast asleep.

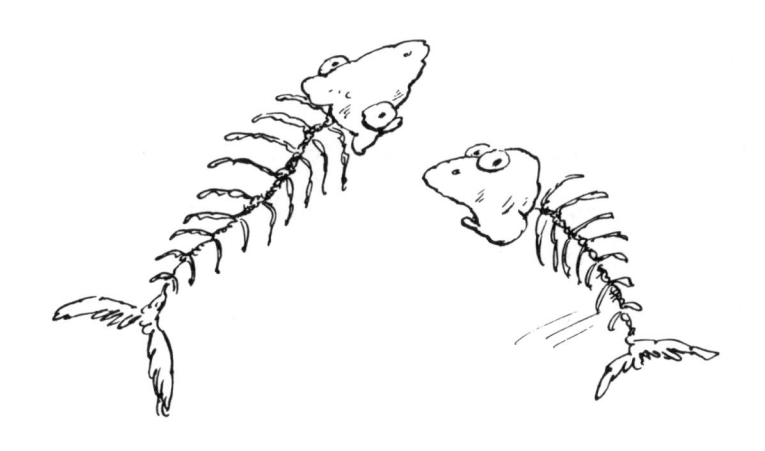

This story is by David Thomson

The Long, Blue Blazer

When I was five, there was a boy in my class who wore a long, blue blazer. He had short arms and short legs and big feet that stuck out from under his long, blue blazer.

He arrived one winter's day. He wandered into the classroom covered in snow and shook hands with the teacher. She said, 'You must be Wilson, the new boy.'

She told him to hang up his things. He took off his cap and his scarf and his mittens. But he wouldn't take off his long, blue blazer.

The teacher asked him to, but he said he was cold, so she let him keep it on.

Later on we did some painting. We all had to put plastic aprons on, but Wilson put his apron on over his long, blue blazer.

I painted my mum in a pink,

flowery dress and Mary painted her mum in green stripy trousers. But Wilson painted his mum in a long, blue blazer.

He ate his school dinner in his long, blue blazer. He did his sums in his long, blue blazer. He even did P.E. in his long, blue blazer.

The teacher asked him to take it off, but he said his mother would be angry if he did, so she let him keep it on.

When it was time to go home, my mum came to fetch me, but nobody came for Wilson. He stood alone in his long, blue blazer, staring up at the sky. The teacher asked him why his mother hadn't come to fetch him. He said she lived too far away.

Wilson walked slowly through the schoolgates, his long, blue blazer dragging in the snow.

The teacher spoke to my mum and I was told to run after Wilson and invite him for tea. That seemed to make him happy. But when my mum asked him to take off his long, blue blazer, he looked as if he was about to cry, so she let him keep it on.

She gave him some steak and kidney pie and sat him on her lap. He put his arms round her and started to cry. He said he was tired.

Mum carried Wilson up to my bedroom and sat him on a chair while she fetched him some pyjamas. When she came back, he'd climbed into my bunkbed in his long, blue blazer and pulled the blankets around him. I slept in the bottom bunk.

Later that night, a loud humming noise woke me up. The wind was making the curtains flap, so I got up to shut the window. I saw green and yellow flashing lights, and there, standing on the windowsill, was Wilson. Suddenly . . . he jumped.

The last I ever saw of him was his long, blue TAIL!

This story is by Jeanne Willis.

Lord of the Golden Umbrellas

The Lord of the Golden Umbrellas, the Wearer of the Crown Shaped like a Temple, the Keeper of the Most Majestic White Elephant, the Wearer of Jade and Pearls, was none other than the King of Siam and he loved his royal cat. She was the colour of clotted cream and her paws were browner than cinnamon, and her eyes were bluer than any corner of the sunlit sky. She sat with elegance upon her silken cushion. She supped from her bowl of beaten silver patterned with jewel-bright enamels. She slept upon the royal pillow and wore a golden necklace. Linked to her necklace was another chain of gold which the King kept looped about a finger. She was his most treasured possession and he called her Precious One.

And she was indeed a valuable cat! Precious One could advise her King upon the affairs of his kingdom, on the growth of his children, a colour for a new robe, a gift for a favourite wife, or food for a feast. And she knew when to speak seriously and when to chat and gossip. All the people of the land knew of Precious One's wisdom, yet, when the King fell ill, no-one thought to consult his cat.

The doctors said, 'It is the heat of the summer which has sickened the Lord of the Golden Umbrellas.' And they advised him to sit in a glass room which was to be lowered into the lake. 'It will be cool in the room and

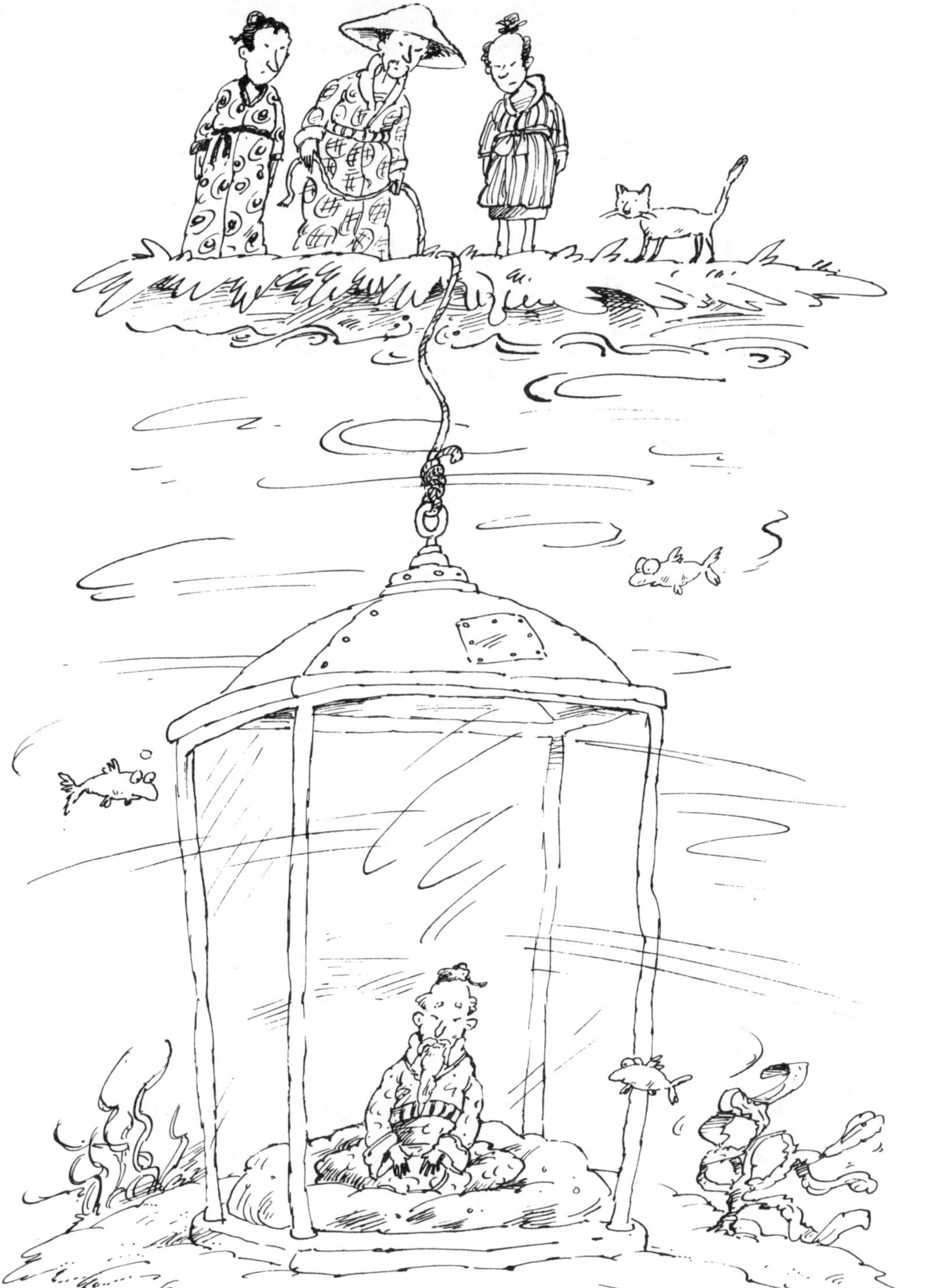

you can watch the fish swim by,' they told him.

However, this treatment did not improve the King's health. As each day passed he grew paler and weaker. The doctors shook their heads. 'Someone must be poisoning His Majesty,' they whispered. 'Set guards to watch over the royal goblet and His Majesty's golden plate.'

Now the King had many wives and each wife loved him well. They took it upon themselves to guard his food and drink. Alas, all fell asleep during the early hours of the morning, when the dark of night turned to the pale grey of dawn. And alas, the King's health grew worse. It was likely that he would die.

'I will guard my Lord of the Golden Umbrellas,' spoke up Precious One. 'I shall watch over his goblet and his plate.'

'You will not be able to stay awake,' the doctors said. 'You sleep more often than a person. That is the habit of a cat, even one as noble as yourself.'

'Trust me,' said Precious One. 'Trust me!'

She sprang to the table to lie close to the goblet and the plate. And she stayed awake all through that day and through the night. She stayed awake the next day and then another night. It was near to dawn when her eyelids slipped over her weary eyes. It was for a moment only. Precious One shook herself awake.

Again and again her eyes all but closed. She forced them to open wide, fixing her gaze on the goblet and plate. If only she could take a cat-nap, a brief cat-nap to refresh her weariness.

Now, Precious One was wise as well as beautiful, you will remember.

And she uncurled her long tail which had been wrapped about her feet. She twisted its brown tip about the stem of the golden goblet and she held it tightly, very tightly. Then Precious One slept. No-one dared to reach for the goblet. No-one dared approach the golden plate. Precious one would have awakened at once to claw at the wicked hand.

And so days went by. Nights went by. Precious One still clung to the goblet and as each day passed the Lord of the Golden Umbrellas grew stronger. Soon he was completely well from his serious illness. 'Precious One has saved our lord from death by poison,' declared the doctors.

It was never discovered who was trying to kill the King.

'The evil person must have left the kingdom by this time,' his wives

Lord of the Golden Umbrellas

believed. 'Precious One no longer needs to guard the royal goblet and the golden plate.'

The King lifted his cat from the table and placed her in his lap. He stroked down her neck, down her back, down her tail. 'What has happened to your tail, Oh Precious One?' asked the King. 'Its tip is now crooked.'

'That is of no consequence, my Lord,' she mewed, knowing that the long hours grasping the goblet had spoilt the beauty of her tail. 'Let us not think upon it,' she purred.

And her tail tip stayed slightly curved. No amount of smoothing or stroking would straighten it. The same little crooked tip appeared on the tails of Precious One's kittens and every kitten born into the Royal Siamese Cat Family since. You may see such a tail, if you know a cat like Precious One. That same cat will have the grace of a tiger, the sweetness of a lovebird, the beauty of a deer, the quickness of lightning and the wisdom of an elephant. So it is said in Siam.

This story is by Jean Chapman.